Misguiding Lights?

Though this book is designed for group study, it is also intended for your personal enjoyment and spiritual growth. A leader's guide is available from your local bookstore or from your publisher.

MIS GUIDING LIGHTS?

EDITED BY
STEPHEN M. MILLER

Beacon Hill Press of Kansas City
Kansas City, Missouri

Editor
Stephen M. Miller

Editorial Assistant
Rebecca Privett

Editorial Committee
Thomas Mayse
Stephen M. Miller
Carl Pierce
Gene Van Note
Lyle Williams

Copyright 1991

Printed in the United States of America
ISBN: 083-411-2809

Cover design by Paul Franitza, photo by Comstock

Bible Credits

Unless otherwise indicated, all Scripture references are from *The Holy Bible, New International Version,* copyright ⓒ 1973, 1978, 1984 by the International Bible Society, and are used by permission of Zondervan Bible Publishers.

Quotation from the *New American Standard Bible* (NASB), ⓒ The Lockman Foundation, 1960, 1962, 1963, 1968, 1971, 1972, 1973, 1975, 1977, is used by permission.

Quotation from *The New Testament in Modern English* (Phillips), Revised Edition ⓒ J. B. Phillips, 1958, 1960, 1972, is used by permission of the Macmillan Publishing Co.

King James Version (KJV).

15   14   13   12   11   10

CONTENTS

99802

1

The Appeal of Cults

By RONALD ENROTH

Ronald Enroth is professor of sociology at Westmont College, Santa Barbara, Calif., and author or editor of several books about cults. His most recent book is Evangelizing the Cults (Servant Publications).

JIM ARDMORE was a burned-out, 25-year-old social worker. He was frustrated with his job, turned off by conventional religion, yet curious about meditation and the other trappings of Eastern religion. I remember Jim telling me what it felt like when he first got zapped by the touch of a guru. The "energy" Jim felt in this touch that initiated him into the Divine Light Mission transformed his life.

"I was just loaded with love. It was just pure love, really strong. And it kept getting stronger, more intense. Tears were streaming down my cheeks

The emotion was just flowing. I hadn't cried since I was in the first grade."

Jim had started on a cultic pilgrimage that would alter the course of his career and his life. After this initiation, Jim didn't return to work for over a week. "I was just higher than a kite. I was God talking to God, standing on God, breathing God." When Jim finally did return to work, he stayed only a few days and then resigned.

During the following months, Jim meditated for hours each day. Extended meditation, designed to empty the mind, can actually lower a person's IQ. (You can read more about this in the chapter on Transcendental Meditation, by David Haddon.) Jim's mind turned to jelly beans. He had been a college graduate with special skills in math, yet he literally lost the ability to add and subtract.

"I could not balance a checkbook," he said. "I was always spaced out. I was at the point where I would accept almost anything my leaders told me, since I was not capable of questioning anything.

"One day I was asked whether I would die for the guru. And when I replied I would, I was told I was making progress quickly. In fact, if the guru had instructed me to murder my mother at that time, I would have done so without hesitation, confident I was doing her a favor."

Why would a bright, young man like Jim join an extremist religious cult? What is it about these new, high-demand religions that so effectively suck people in? Are the folks who sign on emotionally unstable? Do they realize what they are getting into? Are they running away from something?

LURES FOR NORMAL PEOPLE

People who belong to cults are, for the most part, people just like you and me. They may be your neighbors, friends, or even relatives. Most are white and middle-class, with a year or two of college and a desire to find happiness and self-fulfillment. Most have nominal religious backgrounds. As children they were exposed to some Sunday School or church experience, but they didn't come from deeply religious families.

Why are these normal people drawn into what are sometimes pretty bizarre cults?

Theology is not the drawing card. You don't have to be a psychiatrist or a theologian to conclude that cults are meeting needs. People would not be flocking to gurus, self-improvement groups, and pseudo-Christian cults if something weren't happening. Some Christians think people join cults primarily for religious or theological reasons. That's not true.

After two decades of interviewing hundreds of ex-cult members, my research has convinced me that doctrinal reasons are often secondary to the personal and social reasons.

The story of a young man named John illustrates this. He was dating a girl who had gotten involved with a cultic group through a friend of hers. She invited John to join too.

"She kept bugging me to join," John told me. "But I'm a skeptic and don't do things unless I want to. One day her birthday was approaching, and she said to me, 'Well, you know what you can get me for my birthday?' 'No, what?' I answered. 'Come to the meeting.' So I went to the meeting, and everyone was so incredibly nice to me that it made me think. It was unbelievable. I never had known people who were so nice to me. I liked what I saw. About a week later I went back, and the week after that I went back again, and I kept going."

It can be as simple as that.

The lure of friends, Good Samaritans, and seminars. People are recruited in three basic ways: (1) by a friend or relative who is already a member of the cult, (2) by someone unknown to the recruit who befriends or persuades him, or (3) through a cult-sponsored activity, such as a seminar, Bible study, lecture, or free consultation.

Cults often promise more than they can deliver. They not only offer solutions to spiritual dilemmas but often hold out the promise of increased communication skills, healing of mind and body, personal happiness and prosperity, and even the resolution of international political conflict. *Time* magazine recently carried a two-page advertisement, claiming that transcendental meditation (TM) was responsible for the new dawning of happiness, peace, and freedom in many countries of the world.* And later, when Iraq invaded Kuwait, TM's guru Maharishi Mahesh Yogi called on the world to use meditation to solve the crisis.

Wounded people are vulnerable. Former cult members have told me their recruitment strategy included targeting people who were experiencing problems in their life. One person told me how his group would wait outside university counseling centers to "pick off the lambs" as they left the building.

Cults look for people who are feeling depressed, lonely, unloved.

One young woman told me about her troubled background, which included child abuse. She told me she struggled with what she felt were demonic powers in her life. Then she met a small band of people who seemed able to help her.

"When I got to this place," she said, "everybody was so happy, and all the people were so full of love. I had never seen anything like that."

The people accepted her just as she was.

"When I got into that environment of total love and acceptance, it just sucked me in."

Stressed-out people are vulnerable. Many people who get involved with cults report that when they were recruited, they were experiencing stress. Usually, they were undergoing some kind of personal transition: between high school and college, between jobs, between marriages.

People are also vulnerable when they are facing financial pressures, academic problems, the loss of a loved one, or a

---

*March 19, 1990.

move to a new city. Young adults often cite communication problems with parents or the breakup with a boyfriend or girlfriend.

THE SUBSTITUTE FAMILY

Cults not only direct their energy to the spiritual concerns of their members but also address a whole range of human problems. And one way many cults attempt to solve some of the common problems of life—like a lack of encouragement and money—is to become a kind of substitute family for the people.

We see this notion of "family" in the names of some cults: the Christ Family, the Children of God, the Love Family. Some leaders are addressed with parental titles: Father David (David Berg of the Children of God) and Father Moon (Sun Myung Moon of the Unification church).

Religious cults, especially those structured as communes, often operate in an environment sealed off from the rest of the world. The "family" provides food, shelter, and all the necessities of life. In fact, the cult frequently provides jobs for the members and sometimes arranges marriages.

People who have what psychologists call "dependency needs" are attracted to this kind of security available in cults.

As one young woman told me, "I had just graduated from college and was unsure about venturing out into that big world. I didn't like making decisions. In the cult, the decisions were made for me by the leadership. I didn't really have to face the world, reality. This group was my security."

The father figure. An important drawing card for many cult recruits is the charismatic, authoritarian personality of the leader. The newer cults often have living leaders who inspire, comfort, and provide a sense of direction for the converts.

Cult leaders not only give spiritual guidance and convince followers that their version of the "truth" is unique but also create and enforce the everyday rules of the community.

Yet the converts don't see these people as controlling, manipulative deceivers. The members see their leaders as strong, idealistic, caring pathfinders who can dispel confusion and uncertainty about all areas of life. A god in the flesh is easier for some people to believe in.

In those cults where the founder is no longer alive, his influence is reinforced by continual reference to past exploits and through the sacred writings of the deceased person.

For example, the Church of Scientology has taken extraordinary measures to preserve the writings of founder L. Ron Hubbard. The literature is stored in two deep vaults at the end of a 670-foot tunnel in New Mexico. The tunnel itself is encased in thick concrete and has four doors designed to be maintenance-free for at least 1,000 years. Hubbard's taped lectures are being recorded onto gold compact discs.

Though people are not primarily attracted to cults because of the cult's theology, converts are soon indoctrinated. So Christians who want to win these people for Christ must recognize those who join cultic movements are convinced of the truth their group teaches. Cult members need information to help them identify the false teaching they have adopted. This calls for caring, patient, informed witness on the part of Christians.

That's part of what this book is about. We're hoping to give you a little insight into what a few of the cults and other religions teach.

One discovery I believe you'll make is that these "other gospels" reflect a society that has increasingly distanced itself from the God of the Bible. Cults are poised, ready to take advantage of the spiritual vacuum.

A famous English writer from several decades ago, G. K. Chesterton, once said that when people stop believing in God, it isn't that they believe in nothing. It's that they believe in anything.

Mormonism

AT A GLANCE

HOW IT STARTED

Joseph Smith, a young farmer in New York, started the Church of Jesus Christ of Latter-day Saints (LDS) in 1830. Members, also known as Mormons, were forced to move west because of their unusual beliefs, such as the belief one man could have several wives. (This practice ended in 1890.) They settled in Utah in 1847.

KEY ATTRACTIONS

The Mormon church emphasizes traditional family values and provides many activities to encourage this. Mormonism also presents a positive view of humanity and teaches that almost everyone will gain a place in heaven. It also claims to be God's only true church, with the authority to act for Him.

WHERE IT PARTS COMPANY WITH CHRISTIANITY

Mormonism teaches God is married and was once a man. Humans are literally the children of God. As the same species, we each have the potential to become a god. The Mormons have three extra volumes of "holy" scripture besides the Bible. They consider these newer scriptures more reliable.

STATUS TODAY

In about 160 years the Mormon church has grown to over 7 million members worldwide. One out of 60 people in the U.S. is a Mormon. There are 35,000 Mormon missionaries who bring in about 300,000 converts a year.

Sandra Tanner is a great-great-granddaughter of Brigham Young, the Mormon who led his people to Utah after the death of Joseph Smith, who started Mormonism. Since 1983, Sandra and her husband have directed Utah Lighthouse Ministry in Salt Lake City. The nonprofit organization helps Mormons find salvation through Christ.

Mormons:
The Only True Church

By SANDRA TANNER

LAST SUMMER two women in their mid-30s came to my office and asked if I had time to talk to them about Mormonism.

Jean was a Christian. Rose was a convert to Mormonism.

The two friends had been talking for several weeks about Jesus and the Bible. Rose kept insisting she believed in Christ as her Savior, so she couldn't understand why Jean felt the Mormon church was not a Christian church.

Eventually, Jean convinced Rose to visit with me so I could explain why I left the Latter-day Saints (LDS). I told Rose that all Christian churches believe in one absolute God, who has always existed as God. The Mormon church doesn't. It teaches that God was once a human on another earth, and that He progressed to the position of God over just our earth.

Mormons also believe God is married and has a mother and father. These divine parents are gods over another earth, with grandparents who rule over yet other earths.

Rose objected. She said that though the LDS teaches we can become gods over other earths, she didn't think it taught there were many gods before our Father God.

I asked her if she had heard the Mormons saying, "As man is, God once was; as God is, man may become." She said she had. I pointed out that this couplet taught the very point I had just made.

I then showed her in the LDS handbook *Gospel Principles*

13

that it says "our heavenly parents" have "resurrected bodies." The book adds, "This is the way our Heavenly Father became a God. Joseph Smith taught, 'It is the first principle of the Gospel to know for a certainty the character of God ... he was once a man like us; ... God himself, the Father of us all, dwelt on an earth, the same as Jesus Christ himself did.'"

I pointed out to her that obviously there had to be a different god in charge of that earth when our god was still just a human being.

Rose sat there quietly for a moment, then replied, "I never really thought about it before."

I then told her how, when I was a young Mormon, a Christian challenged me to read Isaiah 43:10, "I am he: before me there was no God formed, neither shall there be after me" (KJV).* And Isaiah 44:8, "Is there a God beside me? yea, there is no God; I know not any."

These same thoughts are repeated time and again in Isaiah. When I read these verses, I could see they ruled out the Mormon teaching that man has the potential to progress to godhood.

Jean entered the discussion then and told me she had been trying to explain to Rose about salvation by grace. Rose couldn't see that the LDS church was teaching anything contrary to the Bible about salvation.

I again took my copy of *Gospel Principles* and showed her that LDS Apostle Boyd Packer taught that Christ's atonement was only the beginning of our quest for eternal life. The Lord's atonement was not the complete, final payment spoken of in Ephesians 2.

Apostle Packer used a parable to explain the Mormon concept of the Atonement. He told of a man who, fearing imprisonment due to his huge debt, found a friend to pay his bill: "The mediator turned then to the debtor, 'If I pay your debt, will you accept me as your creditor?'

---

*All scriptures in this chapter are from the King James Version.

" 'Oh yes, yes,' cried the debtor. 'You saved me from prison and showed mercy to me.'

" 'Then,' said the benefactor, 'you will pay the debt to me and I will set the terms. It will not be easy, but it will be possible. I will provide a way.' "

This, I told Rose, doesn't sound like grace. It sounds more like refinancing.

Mormons view the Atonement as the door through which we must pass to gain entrance to the stairway of personal acts of righteousness. By doing good deeds, we become worthy to live with God.

LEARNING TO SPEAK THE LINGO

One of the problems Christians have in witnessing to LDS people and in learning what they believe is that both groups use many of the same religious words. But the meaning is very different.

The Mormon church has redefined most words Christians use to explain their faith.

When a Christian speaks of being saved or of the assurance of heaven, a Mormon will readily agree. But the average Christian doesn't realize that to the Mormon, "saved by grace" means everyone will be resurrected through Christ. Mormons believe the resurrected masses will be placed in different levels of heaven. The more good works the people have done, the higher in heaven they get to go.

All those who reach heaven will live forever. And, in the Mormon view, most people—even non-Mormons—will reach heaven. But not everyone will have what Mormons refer to as "eternal life." To the Mormon, eternal life is more than immortality. It is the ability to eternally procreate and give life. So, contrary to John 3:36 and Luke 20:35, Mormons say eternal life is the ability to live forever in the family unit. This means producing millions of spirit children to inhabit the earth they will form.

Only those who are faithful Mormons, married in a Mormon temple, will be granted this "eternal life."

As Rose, Jean, and I talked, Rose began to understand how different the LDS teachings were from the standard Christian view. As she left, she said she would continue to meet with Jean and study the Bible.

Rose is typical of the 300,000 people who will convert to Mormonism this year. She is a bright, middle-class woman, looking for security for her family. But she is not well-informed about the teachings of the church she joined.

What attracts people to the Mormon church are its family-oriented programs, its positive view of human nature, and its teaching that almost everyone will be saved and will live in some level of heaven.

IN SEARCH OF THE TRUE CHURCH

Mormonism also appeals to people confused by the many different religions and disturbed that all Christians do not belong to the same denomination. Such people relate to Joseph Smith's search for the only true church.

Joseph Smith, founder of Mormonism, was born in 1805 and grew up on a farm in upstate New York. As a youngster, he and his family were involved in folk magic. They used magical seer stones and divining rods to look for buried treasure, underground minerals, and lost items.

Smith said that during this period he became concerned about which church he should join. So he took the problem to God in prayer.

In *Pearl of Great Price,* a book Mormons treat as scripture, Smith told of attending revivals in his neighborhood where: "Some were contending for the Methodist faith, some for the Presbyterian, and some for the Baptist."

Faced with this dilemma, Smith decided only God could tell him which one was right: "So, in accordance with this, my determination to ask of God, I retired to the woods to make the attempt . . . When the light rested upon me, I saw two personages, whose brightness and glory defy all description, standing above me in the air. One of them spake unto me, calling me by name and said, pointing to the other—This is My Beloved Son. Hear Him!

"My object in going to inquire of the Lord was to know which of all the sects was right, that I might know which to join . . . I was answered that I must join none of them, for they were all wrong; and the Personage who addressed me said that all their creeds were an abomination in his sight; that those professors were all corrupt."

On the basis of this vision, Mormons argue that God has rejected all other churches, and that no one outside the Mormon church has the authority to baptize or to act for God. They also point to this vision as proof that God the Father and Jesus Christ both have physical bodies.

Smith also claimed that in 1827 an angel delivered to him a set of gold plates. These plates contained the history of Lehi and his family, who migrated from Jerusalem in 600 B.C. and brought civilization to the American continents. The *Book of Mormon* is supposed to be the translation of these plates.

In 1830 Smith founded his church and printed the *Book of Mormon*. Over the next 14 years he issued scores of revelations printed under the title *Doctrine and Covenants*. He also produced two other sacred writings, the Book of Moses and the Book of Abraham, printed under the title *Pearl of Great Price*. Mormons consider these three books, along with the King James Version of the Bible, their holy scripture.

Of the four books, Mormons consider the Bible least reliable. When I have pointed out to them inconsistencies between the Bible and their other books of scripture, their modern writings always take precedence. That's because Mormons believe the church fathers in the early centuries of Christianity changed the text of the Bible, leaving Christians with tainted doctrines.

NEW, IMPROVED MORMON TEACHING

One of the curious aspects of early Mormon history is the repeated revision of Joseph Smith's revelations and church doctrine.

A few months ago Ted, a middle-aged Mormon, visited our bookstore. As we compared beliefs, he insisted that because the Bible is so corrupted, we needed a prophet to give us the clear doctrines of God.

I asked him for an example of mistakes or inaccurate teachings in the Bible—anything that showed evidence the church fathers had tampered with the text. He said the Gospels give different accounts of the Resurrection.

I told him this was not an example of inaccuracy. If three people witness a car wreck, they see it from three different perspectives. So they report it from those three perspectives. The differences in the reports do not mean the testimony is in error or that someone distorted the accounts.

I then asked him how he felt about Joseph Smith rewriting his own revelations. Ted told me he heard there were a few grammatical changes, but they didn't amount to much. I got out a photo reprint of the original printing of Smith's revelations and compared it to later versions. Several sections had undergone major revisions that changed the meaning of the text.

Ted simply responded that he was sure the changes were made for good reasons, and if the prophet changed them, God had approved the changes.

I then reminded Ted that Jesus warned in Matthew 24:11 and 24 there would be false prophets in the last days and that we are to be on guard against those who would lead us astray.

Ted agreed. But he felt he had spiritual confirmation, through prayer, that Joseph Smith was a true prophet.

I asked Ted for a Bible verse that tells me how to determine if someone is a true or false prophet. He mentioned James 1:5, "If any of you lack wisdom, let him ask of God." I told him this verse talks about getting "wisdom," not testing a prophet.

I opened my Bible to Deuteronomy 13 and directed Ted to the warning against anyone claiming to be a prophet who teaches a wrong concept of God. And I showed Ted that Deuteronomy 18 warns against those whose prophecies fail. Next, I turned to Galatians 1:8-9, where Paul warned about those who teach contrary to the teachings of the New Testament.

I explained to Ted that because of this, I could have confidence that God's message in the Bible is the same today as it was for the early Christians. No revisions have been needed. It is thoroughly reliable.

Ted is a good example of the Mormon mind-set. They downgrade the authority of the Bible but accept without question the word of their leaders.

As God gives us opportunity to share our faith in Christ with our Mormon friends, we need to remember that years of false teaching are not usually reversed in one conversation. I've observed that most Mormons who come to Christ have at least one Christian friend witnessing to them for months or years.

We Christians also need to be sensitive to the emotional trauma a Mormon goes through when he leaves that faith for a new life in Christ.

A former Mormon in Idaho expressed it well in a letter she wrote me: "It was a heartbreak for me to learn of all the deception. I cried for days and still refused to believe it until I . . . read for myself the very books you had quoted from. But later when I found the real, biblical Jesus, my joy far outweighed my heartbreak. . . . A tremendous burden has been released from my shoulders when I found the real Jesus."

Jehovah's Witnesses

AT A GLANCE

HOW IT STARTED

Charles Taze Russell, a man with no formal religious training, started a religious magazine called *Zion's Watch Tower*. In 1879 he printed 6,000 copies. Five years later he formed Zion's Watch Tower and Tract Society. Today, 28 million copies of *The Watchtower* are printed each month. This is the official magazine of the Jehovah's Witnesses.

KEY ATTRACTIONS

People are drawn into the Jehovah's Witnesses through an aggressive strategy of door-to-door and street-corner evangelism. Witnesses tell people that joining their organization is the only way to avoid destruction in the coming Battle of Armageddon.

WHERE IT PARTS COMPANY WITH CHRISTIANITY

Jehovah's Witnesses deny many of the key beliefs of Christianity. They deny the Trinity, Christ's deity, His bodily resurrection, His visible second coming, a heavenly home for all believers, and eternal punishment for all who reject Christ.

STATUS TODAY

In the early 1900s, one critic of the Watchtower Society said that when Russell died, the group would "sink into the limbo of things forgotten." Today there are nearly 4 million Jehovah's Witnesses worldwide. Their headquarters is in Brooklyn.

M. Kurt Goedelman is executive director of Personal Freedom Outreach, a nonprofit, nondenominational ministry that studies fringe religious groups. Goedelman lives in St. Louis.

Jehovah's Witnesses:

The View from the Watchtower

By M. KURT GOEDELMAN

PAUL BLIZARD is my friend. He grew up as a third-genera-
tion Jehovah's Witness. His grandfather had joined the Watchtower Society in the early 1900s. Paul's father is still an elder
in a Kingdom Hall.

But several years ago, Paul was excommunicated from
the Jehovah's Witnesses.

It all began shortly after his daughter was born with a
rare blood disease. Paul and his wife already had two boys.
So when Jenny came along, they were excited to have a little
girl to add to the family. But five weeks later, doctors discovered Jenny had started to bleed internally and that her blood
would not clot. She needed an emergency blood transfusion.

This posed a serious spiritual problem for Paul and his
wife. In fact, voluntarily agreeing to the transfusion could get
them excommunicated. That would mean their Witness family
members and friends could no longer have anything to do
with them. Worse, as far as Witnesses were concerned, Paul
and his family would face annihilation after death. There
would be no hope of salvation.

This belief that people must say no to blood transfusions
is unique to Jehovah's Witnesses. The Watchtower has taken

the Old Testament dietary law against eating blood and mis-applied it to blood transfusions.

Many Jehovah's Witnesses have died from curable ail-ments because of this belief. Witnesses have gone to court to block transfusions. Some have even abducted children from hospitals to prevent the transfusion.

Paul and his wife sent the doctors out of the room, then prayed. "I remember thinking," Paul said, "O Jehovah, how can You ask me to make such a decision—a yes or no whether Jenny lives? What kind of God are You?"

But after the prayer, Paul and his wife decided to obey what they believed to be God's law. They told the doctors they would let Jenny die.

Within a few hours, medical authorities got a court order allowing them to treat Jenny. In addition, the state welfare de-partment filed a suit against the Blizards, charging them with child abuse and neglect.

In the meantime, friends contacted the local elders, who rushed to the hospital. "They were relieved to find out there was still time to plan a way to get Jenny out of the hospital before the blood could be administered," Paul said.

"I explained that Jenny would shortly die if I removed her from the machines that were keeping her alive, and I would be charged with murder," Paul said. "They replied, 'That's the chance you have to take. You cannot allow them to give your child blood.'"

Paul refused. Then he ordered the elders to leave. He said he could not allow his child to die this way. "If this is the God I serve," Paul said, "I am through with Him."

The elders left the hospital, upset over Paul's decision. On the way out, one elder replied, "I hope she gets hepatitis from that blood, just to prove that it's bad!"

Jenny survived this crisis. And the Blizards avoided ex-communication. Under Watchtower laws, the Blizards could have been excommunicated only if they had willingly granted permission for the transfusion. But they had resisted.

In the months that followed, Christians came to the Blizard home and provided the family with food, money, and a living testimony of God's compassion. A short while later, Paul and his wife gave their lives to Christ.

On March 3, 1987, six-year-old Jenny went to be with Jesus. At the memorial service, the Blizards reserved the first four pews for the family, in case any decided to come. None did. In those pews sat Paul, his wife, their two boys, and a younger daughter.

Yet through Jenny's illness, the Blizards were able to testify to parents of other terminally ill children about the grace of God. Today, Paul pastors the First Baptist Church in Fairdale, Ky., and directs the Kentucky office of Personal Freedom Outreach, a ministry that teaches Christians about cults and other fringe religious groups.

THE RAISING OF THE WATCHTOWER

Though Christians today know the Jehovah's Witnesses primarily because of the Watchtower's stand on blood transfusions and its aggressive door-to-door evangelism, the organization grew from the seeds of Adventist teaching.

Prophecy about end times was on the mind of Charles Taze Russell when he founded the organization in 1884 in Pennsylvania. He called it Zion's Watch Tower and Tract Society. This was named after the magazine he had started five years earlier, *Zion's Watch Tower.*

Russell believed, as Adventists taught, that Christ had invisibly returned to the earth in 1874. Russell also began predicting the world would end in 1914.

Wealth from his father's clothing business enabled him to publish his magazine and six volumes of a series called "Studies in the Scriptures." Russell, who called himself a pastor, warned that people who studied the Bible without the help of his "Studies" would become spiritually confused.

Russell died in 1916. That was two years after the 1914 date he predicted the bloody Battle of Armageddon would end and the world would become a paradise. A few months after Russell's death, Joseph F. Rutherford, a Missouri lawyer, took over the Watchtower Society.

Rutherford made changes. He replaced some of Russell's beliefs with his own. Then he set 1925 as the new date for the world's end, as we know it. He wrote an average of a book a year, and 300 million copies of his books were published in his lifetime.

Rutherford solidified Russell's membership gains, then weathered mass desertions from the society after his 1925 prophecy failed.

In 1931 he began calling society members Jehovah's Witnesses. Then he launched the society's door-to-door work. During this time he abandoned Russell's teaching that Christ had returned in 1874. Instead, he began teaching Christ had returned in 1914.

Rutherford died in 1942 and was replaced by Nathan H. Knorr. Knorr inherited 65,000 "publishers," or Witnesses who promoted the Watchtower's message. Knorr improved the society's business practices, established theological schools, and published training guides. When he died in 1977, there were 2.25 million Jehovah's Witnesses.

During Knorr's tenure, the society produced its own translation of the Bible. The Watchtower's Bible, completed in 1961, is called the *New World Translation of the Holy Scriptures.* The work was done by five Jehovah's Witness leaders. None of the men held degrees in biblical languages. And only one claimed to be able to read ancient Hebrew and Greek. Biblical scholars today reject the Jehovah's Witness translation as inaccurate. The translation distorts Christian doctrine to suit Watchtower beliefs.

One of these five men was Frederick W. Franz. He was a vice president under Knorr and succeeded him in 1977. Franz helped shape current Watchtower beliefs. In 1966 he wrote a book that implied the world would end in 1975. Jehovah's Witnesses took the book so seriously that some began selling their homes and property. In 1974 the Watchtower praised members who sold their homes and devoted themselves to full-time Watchtower service.

Again, the end failed to arrive, and Watchtower membership dropped sharply. Rumblings and discontent resulted in nearly 30,000 "apostates" being expelled in 1978.

In spite of all the problems the Watchtower Society has endured because of its preoccupation with end times, the theme remains a dominant part of their magazines and books.

APOSTLES OF DENIAL

Author Edmund C. Gruss chose to name his book on Watchtower history and beliefs *Apostles of Denial.* That was a good choice because Jehovah's Witnesses deny most of the key doctrines of the Christian faith.

They deny the Trinity, the deity of Jesus Christ, the person of the Holy Spirit, the bodily resurrection of Christ, His visible second coming, humanity's eternal soul, the existence of hell, and a heavenly home for all believers.

Trinity. Jehovah's Witnesses believe that God exists as one personality they call "Jehovah" or the Father. A recent Watchtower book says, "To worship God on His terms means to reject the Trinity doctrine." Another Jehovah's Witness publication said, "Satan is the originator of the 'Trinity' doctrine."

Jesus. Watchtower denial of the Trinity means Witnesses do not believe in Jesus' deity.

Jehovah's Witnesses believe that before Jesus' life on earth, He was Michael the archangel. They believe Michael gave up his angelic life to be born a human. Witnesses believe that during His life on earth, Jesus was just a man.

Witnesses have creatively interpreted key Bible verses to support these beliefs. John 1:1, speaking about Jesus, says, "In the beginning was the Word, and the Word was with God, and the Word was God." The *New World Translation* reads: "In [the] beginning the Word was, and the Word was with God, and the Word was a god."

Jesus was not *the* God. He was *a* god. Watchtower writers explain, "Since the Bible calls humans angels, even Satan, 'gods,' or powerful ones, the superior Jesus in heaven can properly be called 'a god.'"

The Watchtower repeatedly cites Bible passages about Christ's humanness but ignores or mistranslates verses about His divinity. These include Titus 2:13, "While we wait for the blessed hope—the glorious appearing of our great God and Savior, Jesus Christ." (See also John 20:28 and 2 Peter 1:1.)

The Watchtower limits those who can benefit from Christ's saving work to 144,000 "elect" Christians, of which fewer than 9,000 are alive today. Witnesses believe only these will reign with Jehovah God.

The society teaches that the "nonelect"—those not part of the chosen 144,000—must come to the Watchtower Society for salvation. For them, there is no salvation through Jesus. Salvation depends on their attitude toward the "elect," or anointed. The "chosen" include leaders of the society.

Attitudes that warrant salvation show up in a person's willingness to obey the society's rules and go along with the program. That is part of the reason Witnesses are so aggressive in their door-to-door evangelism and in distributing their literature. They feel they must earn their salvation by showing they have a good attitude toward their leadership.

Elders in the society have the power to excommunicate members and deny them salvation. The society teaches that the saved will enjoy everlasting life in an earthly paradise. The lost will face annihilation. Jehovah's Witnesses do not believe in a place of eternal punishment for unbelievers.

Holy Spirit. The Watchtower teaches there is a Holy Spirit but that He is not divine and is not a person. Witnesses believe the Holy Spirit is a force, somewhat like electricity.

The Watchtower ignores verses about the Spirit's personality and divinity. From Scripture, we know the Spirit has a mind and a will (Romans 8:27; 1 Corinthians 12:11). He has the ability to speak (Acts 13:2-4), teach (John 14:26), pray (Romans 8:26), appoint (Acts 20:28), and bear witness (John 15:26).

The resurrection of Christ. A Christian's hope depends on Christ's resurrection. Paul said in 1 Corinthians 15:14, "If Christ has not been raised, our preaching is useless and so is your faith." Jehovah's Witnesses say they believe in Jesus' resurrection, but they say it was Christ's spirit, not His body, that was raised.

This teaching clashes with the gospel. In John 2:19-21, Jesus said a sign of His authority would be the death and resurrection of His body. In Luke 24:36-43 Jesus offered to the disciples His physical body as proof of the Resurrection.

The Watchtower's teaching about Christ's resurrection fits perfectly with their teaching about Christ's second coming. Jehovah's Witnesses believe Christ returned in 1914, but most people don't know He returned because Jesus doesn't have a physical body.

This teaching, however, doesn't mesh very well with Revelation 1:7, "Look, he is coming with the clouds, and every eye will see him."

Holidays. Jehovah's Witnesses refuse to observe religious and secular holidays. They believe Christmas and Easter celebrations grew out of pagan practices. They consider birthdays, Mother's Day, and Father's Day as creature worship—a kind of idol worship. Even national holidays are off limits, because they encourage loyalty to a government instead of loyalty to Jehovah.

This ban on holidays serves one more purpose. It isolates Jehovah's Witnesses from society. Isolation is a practice common to many cults.

HOW TO WITNESS TO A WITNESS

Jesus died to save Jehovah's Witnesses as much as He died for anyone else. Christians need to tell them that. Here are a few suggestions I would make about how to witness to a Witness.

Witness with love. Love must be the primary motive for our witnessing. Our motive should not be to prove we are right and they are wrong. Winning an argument is not enough. We need a compassion that realizes that the Jehovah's Witnesses who come to our door are there because they want God's favor.

These are people who need to hear about God's grace, freely given.

Contrast the Watchtower's message and the Christian gospel. Ask the Witnesses what their central message is. They will most likely tell of impending doom for the world.

Then tell the Witness that the gospel message is one of hope. The Good News is about the salvation we can experience, because of the death, burial, and resurrection of Jesus Christ.

Outline the gospel preached by the apostles (1 Corinthians 15:1-4; 1 Peter 1:3; Colossians 1:22-23; 2 Timothy 2:8; and 1 Corinthians 1:23). Explain that the penalty for preaching a gospel different from the apostles' is eternal condemnation (Galatians 1:8-9).

Look at the context of scriptures they use. Be alert for misinterpretation and hopscotching through the Bible. Call their attention to the setting of the passages, when they are quoting isolated verses out of context. To do this, read the verses before and after the cited verse.

Also, use a generally accepted version of the Bible. The Watchtower's *New World Translation* misinterprets many passages.

Mention that prophecies of Witness leaders have not come true. The Watchtower Society claims to be Jehovah's prophet on earth. But Deuteronomy 18:20-22 says the predictions of true prophets happen as prophesied. Yet, Armageddon has not come.

Describe your new life in Christ. Tell the Jehovah's Witness how you became a Christian and what it is like to be one. Use scripture. Stress that the Bible says a person can be saved only by accepting Christ as Lord and Savior.

Give the Jehovah's Witness Christian literature. After your talk, give the Witness some tracts that explain the gospel message. Organizations like the one I direct provide tracts specifically for members of the Watchtower Society.

Invite the Witness to read the literature and check the Bible references. As the Witness is leaving, tell him you will be praying for him, and then do it.

Islam

AT A GLANCE

HOW IT GOT STARTED

Muhammad, born about A.D. 570, began preaching Islam in Mecca, a city in what is now Saudi Arabia. Under persecution he fled to another city where he and his followers set up a religious community in 622.

KEY ATTRACTIONS

Islam, which means "submission to God," teaches there is one God of all people. The Muslim faith gives clear guidance for all of life, has a simple theology, and claims to be the final religion that fulfills the promises of both Judaism and Christianity.

WHERE IT PARTS COMPANY WITH CHRISTIANITY

Muslims believe Jesus was a human prophet, like Muhammad. They also believe Jesus was not God's Son, was not crucified, and did not secure salvation for sinners. In addition, they believe the Bible has been corrupted by changes, and that God provided additional revelation after the Bible was written.

STATUS TODAY

There are close to 1 billion Muslims, worldwide, and 3-5 million in the United States. With the decline of colonialism in Asia and Africa, Islam is growing especially fast there and winning converts from other faiths.

Matt Zahniser is professor of world religions, Asbury Theological Seminary, Wilmore, Ky.

Islam:
Where God Is Great

By MATT ZAHNISER

al-LAA-hoo AK-bar. al-LAA-hoo AK-bar. al-LAA-hoo AK-bar. al-LAA-hoo AK-bar.

With this fourfold chant, which means "God is great," Ismail (is-maa-EEL) summoned 25 believers for noon prayers.

The language was Arabic. The prayers were Islamic. But the place was not Cairo or Baghdad. And Ismail hailed from neither Turkey nor Iran. He was an American Muslim calling fellow Muslims together for prayer in Lexington, Ky.

Five of my comparative religion students and I visited this house of worship to learn about the Muslim faith. We entered this modest two-story brick house through the back door. We passed the taps where men splashed water on their faces, hands, arms, and feet, ritually cleansing themselves in preparation for worship. And we took off our shoes, then stepped quietly into the place of prayer.

As I listened to Ismail's call to prayer and smelled the pungent odor of water on brick and cement, mixed with the faint aroma of garlic, my memory swept me back to Egypt, where I had lived for over a year. But this was Lexington.

As Ismail chanted on, I translated in my mind: "I testify that there is no god but God. I testify that there is no god but God."

We took our seats, sitting cross-legged on the wall-to-wall carpet that covered the simple room in which all the Muslims would assemble in neat lines to pray. Ismail went on: "I testify

31

that Muhammad is the Messenger of God. I testify that Muhammad is the Messenger of God."

Before he finished, and the others began to pray, he chanted: "Come to prayer, come to prayer. Come to success, come to success. God is great, God is great. There is no god but God."

"Only one God exists. And He is infinitely great." I thought about these words as I watched the faithful at prayer. I knew that Christian Arabs call God "Allah," just as Muslims do. I knew that *muslim* in Arabic means "one who surrenders." And I remembered my own surrender to God at the age of 18. I wanted so much to agree with these sincere believers.

But I could not. One sentence Ismail had chanted expressed the gulf between these Muslims and me. I could not say with Ismail, "Muhammad is the Messenger of God." "I believe in God, and I respect Muhammad," I said to myself, "but I cannot accept him as the messenger of God."

WHO WAS MUHAMMAD?

Who was this man who made Ismail a Muslim, but whom I could not accept?

One night in A.D. 610, according to Muslim tradition, Muhammad ibn Abdullah (mo-HAM-ed I-ben ab-DUL-la), a camel caravan leader from the Arabian city of Mecca, went to a cave to meditate and pray. Although he had done this on many other nights, this time Muhammad heard a voice saying to him, "Recite!" After he protested and resisted the command, he finally opened his mouth. Words began to come—not his own words, but, according to Muslim belief, the very words of God.

Muhammad became a fiery preacher in the markets of Mecca. He warned everyone to surrender to the will of the one God. And he passed on what the voice had told him: those who served gods other than the one true God and those who acted unjustly would not escape the fires of hell. The leaders of Mecca stopped their ears against such preaching.

They severely persecuted his followers, even beating and killing some. So when a city to the north of Mecca opened its gates to Muhammad and his followers, the prophet and his disciples migrated.

Here Muhammad became a statesman. He set up in that city, called Medina (ma-DEE-na), the City of the Prophet, a community guided by the messages he continued to receive. Sometimes he heard a message to be preached, at other times a word of encouragement. Sometimes he heard and repeated a solution to a problem or a resolution for a dispute. At other times he recited a story of a former prophet or explained the story.

When Muhammad died in 632, the messages and recitations died with him. But his followers collected them into a book about three-fourths the length of the New Testament. The book is called the Qur'an (coor-ON). Muslims believe that the Qur'an, which means recitation, is the absolute word of God.

By the time Muhammad died, all the people of Arabia had either accepted the prophet and his revelations or had been driven from the region. Before Muhammad had been dead for a century, the armies of this new faith had created a great empire. It stretched from Arabia east to India and west across North Africa to the border between Spain and France.

Today Muhammad's followers number almost 1 billion worldwide. The country with the greatest number of Muslims is Indonesia. It has more than 100 million believers. Some of the other countries with large Muslim populations include India, Pakistan, the Soviet Union, Turkey, Iran, and Egypt.

Here in my own country, at least 3 million people embrace the faith of Muhammad and the Qur'an.

And in this house in Lexington, my students and I sat with 25 Muslims from five countries. After the prayers ended, many gathered around us to talk. They seemed eager to share their faith and showed a firm grasp of its details.

KEY MUSLIM BELIEFS

God. God the Almighty Creator is merciful, forgiving, and just. No god or godlike being other than God exists. God, who controls everything, hears the prayers of His creatures and will come to their aid. He gives guidance to His creatures, and they must obey. God rewards those who obey Him and punishes those who do not. The one unforgivable sin is to treat any other thing or being as though it were a god.

Angels. Though God created humans from earth and gave them free will, He created angels from light to obey Him instinctively. Angels protect humans, keep God's records, deliver God's messages, and administer God's punishment. Two angels are assigned to each person throughout life, keeping a record of all we say and do.

Sacred books. God gives guidance through books revealed to prophets. God gave to Moses the Torah (the first five books of our Bible—Genesis through Deuteronomy). He gave to David the Psalms, and to Jesus the Gospel. But Jews and Christians allowed their books to be corrupted by changes, so the Bible is no longer reliable.

God gave the Qur'an to Muhammad in perfect, infallible Arabic. Because Muhammad was illiterate, he could not have composed such a book. Therefore, the Qur'an represents a miracle of God's grace. Though we can translate the message into other languages, the Qur'an is the word of God only in its Arabic form.

Prophets. Throughout history God sent prophets to guide people to the right path. Among these prophets were people familiar to Jews and Christians: Adam, Noah, Abraham, Moses, David, and Jesus. All these prophets proclaimed a message, as did Muhammad. But Muhammad's message was the final message, and he the final prophet. This is because God directed only Muhammad's message to all humans. His message covers all human situations and remains to this day accurate and uncorrupted. Muslims have also preserved a record of Muhammad's deeds and sayings, which provide additional guidance for all people.

Final judgment. In the last days believers and unbelievers alike will be resurrected for a Day of Judgment. Some will be assigned to hell and others to heaven.

God permits Satan, a fallen angel, to tempt people, making life a testing period for humans. How people respond to testing will affect their eternal destiny. Believers can never be sure of their destiny because it lies in the hands of God. But God will weigh their good deeds against their bad deeds, with good deeds outweighing bad deeds 10 to 1.

God's will. Everything that happens takes place only if God wills. Because human beings do not know what God has planned for them, they need to do their best to do what is right. Then, when they have done their best, they should accept whatever happens as the will of God. One devout Muslim at the Lexington mosque told us, "If, after sincerely doing my best to obey God, I discover at the judgment that He has assigned me to hell, at least I will know that I did all that I could."

DUTIES OF A MUSLIM

The Muslims who met with us singled out five pillars of religious duty as the foundation for the Muslim way of life.

Declare the faith. A Muslim must sincerely believe and say the Word of Witness: "There is no god but God; and Muhammad is the apostle of God."

Pray. Muslims offer formal prayer to God five times each day: daybreak, noon, afternoon, sundown, and after dark. The words of the prayers come mostly from the Qur'an. That sacred book also prescribes the bodily postures for prayer: standing, bowing, placing the forehead on the ground in prostration, and resting back on one's legs in a kneeling position.

Fast. During the month of Ramadan (RA-ma-don), in which Muhammad first received the Qur'an, Muslims fast from daybreak to nightfall. During the long hours of the fast, the faithful abstain from all food, drink, smoking, and sexual contact.

Because the Muslim year contains only 354 days, instead of our 365, Ramadan begins 11 days earlier every year. When the month occurs in the summer, Ramadan's 15-hour days make fasting a hard discipline.

Help the poor. Every year, Muslims give a percentage of their possessions to the community treasury, for distribution to the poor. Though the percentage differs for some possessions, generally it amounts to 2½ percent of the total worth of a person's wealth at the end of the year. Muslims give alms in addition to this required "poor tax."

Make a pilgrimage. Islam requires each Muslim, once in a lifetime, to make a pilgrim journey to the holy city of Mecca in Saudi Arabia. The pilgrimage takes place in the first third of the 12th month of the Muslim year.

On the climactic ninth day of the month the Muslims stand on the mountain of Arafat and listen to a sermon like the last one preached by their prophet. The next day, Muslims on pilgrimage and around the world observe a feast, which like many of the rites of the pilgrimage, relates to the life of Abraham. It was Abraham who, at God's command, left his home and traveled to where God directed him.

JESUS IN THE QUR'AN

Almost always when the Muslims host my students and me, they talk about Jesus before they open up the discussion for questions. They insist that all Muslims must believe in Jesus.

The Qur'an urges Muslims to believe in Jesus (2:136, 2:285).* And the Qur'an tells Muslims who Jesus was: the Messiah (3:45), a word from God (3:45), born of a virgin

---

*The references are to chapter *(surah)* and verse *(ayah)* of the Qur'an.

(3:47), one who spoke from the cradle, healed the blind, and the leper, raised the dead, and made a clay bird fly (3:49).

But the Qur'an also teaches that Jesus was not the Son of God (5:75), that He was not divine (5:116-18), and that He did not die for the sins of the world (4:157).

Clearly the Qur'an presents a different Jesus from the Jesus of the Gospels. The Muslim Jesus is a prophet, like Muhammad. It was to Jesus that God gave a book called the Gospel to reveal God's will to people.

My students and I tried to help the Muslims see what the New Testament teaches—that God sent Jesus so we could know God, not just know God's will. Our Jesus was far more than a prophet who guides us. He saves us and makes us friends with God.

Our Muslim hosts insisted that humans cannot know God. "Since nothing we know resembles God in any way," they explained, "nothing exists that can help us know God. But by means of the Qur'an we can know God's will for us."

We replied that our Book, the Bible, gives us guidance for our lives, but it also leads us to Jesus, through whom we come to know God personally. The person, Muhammad, gave Muslims a book by which they believe they can know God's will. Our Book, the Bible, leads us to a person, Jesus, through whom we can come to know God.

As we put on our shoes and left the Muslim house of worship, the call to prayer echoed in my thoughts. "God is great. There is no god but God." The truth that this God had made himself known to me personally through His Son, Jesus, is the greatest of His great deeds. After doing for us what He did through Jesus, how could God then simply send a messenger with a book?

My students and I failed to convince our hosts they could know God through the Jesus of the New Testament.

Even now, as I think about how difficult it is to make Christ known to our Muslim friends, my memory takes me back almost 30 years to another Ismail I had known as a graduate student. I met Ismail at a party my church gave for international students. Ismail was an Iraqi Muslim doing graduate work in America.

The two of us became good friends. When a small church invited me to come and preach, I invited Ismail to go with me. He gladly accepted.

After I concluded the service, we both spent a happy time visiting with the congregation outside the church. When I got back to my car, Ismail was already seated there, weeping. When I asked him why he was crying, he said, "It is so wonderful to be with people who love God." The people at the church had touched his heart.

Maybe that is the answer. If Muslims can see the love of God in us, perhaps they will be willing to take another look at Jesus.

5

Buddhism

AT A GLANCE

HOW IT GOT STARTED

Siddhartha Gautama, born in northern India in 563 B.C., founded the religion. He became Buddha, "the enlightened one," after meditating 49 days under a tree.

KEY ATTRACTIONS

People are attracted to Buddhism partly because it promises peace, both in the person and in the world. It works to change the world for the better. People also are drawn to the religious devotion they see among Buddhists.

WHERE IT PARTS COMPANY WITH CHRISTIANITY

It is the world's only major religion that does not teach there is a living God. Buddhists believe in reincarnation, and that bad experiences in this life are caused by actions in past lives. The goal of the human soul is to reach nirvana. There, human personality and consciousness are absorbed into the universe.

STATUS TODAY

Buddhism is experiencing worldwide revival. There are over 300 million Buddhists. In America, there are 2 million who worship in 600 temples. The most zealous and fastest-growing branch in America is the Nichiren Shoshu Academy, with about 300,000.

James Stephens was a member of the Buddhist Nichiren Shoshu Academy for 14 years and is a graduate of their school. He is now director of Sonrise Center for Buddhist Studies in Pasadena, Calif. This is a ministry that conducts research and training to convert Buddhists to the Christian faith.

Buddhism:
The Enlightened Ones
By JAMES C. STEPHENS

WHEN I WAS A CHILD growing up in a small, rural town in Montana, I remember attending Sunday School for about two years. My parents, however, had other pressing concerns in raising our family and attended only rarely. I can't ever remember discussing spiritual matters at the dinner table.

At least not until I became a Buddhist in college.

During those growing-up years, I came to realize that a lot of people thought church was important. But very few seemed to take their religion seriously during the rest of the week. My parents, for example, wanted their children to learn about God. But they didn't live a life that showed us how to worship the God we talked about in Sunday School.

By the time I was a senior in high school, my family had moved to California. And I had a lot of questions about spiritual issues: why I was alive, where I would go after I died. It was a heavy time for me. And the only person I found in school who seemed interested in spiritual things was my locker partner, Russ. He was excited about his newfound faith in Buddhism and chanting. But that seemed too bizarre for me.

After high school, I moved back to the state of my childhood and enrolled at the University of Montana. It was there, during a course in psychology, I became intrigued by Eastern religions. That semester left me disoriented and homesick, so I migrated back home to California, where I enrolled in a local

41

university. I soon found that many of my friends, even some of the very conservative ones, had gotten interested in Eastern philosophy.

Then, in one of my classes, I ran into my former locker partner, Russ. This time I was interested in what he had to say about his religion. He told me if you want to change the problems in society, you must first change yourself. Well, that made sense to me.

"How do you do that?" I asked. He explained that chanting produces vibrations that help us get in harmony with the basic components of the universe. Then he invited me to give it a try, since I didn't have anything to lose. A couple of days later he gave me some magazines about Buddhism, which explained how scientific it all was.

As I read the articles and thought more seriously about this philosophy, it seemed reasonable that the answers to life's tough questions would come from the Orient. After all, their civilization had been around a lot longer than ours. And Buddhism had been around long before Christianity.

Within two weeks I was attending meetings on Buddhism. What a different experience. The chanting in these meetings sounded like angels singing in the heavens. There were people from many different races. And the smell of incense added to the mystery of it all. Could this be the answer to the problems we were facing as a planet?

For the next 14 years I practiced Buddhism, zealously converting over 54 people to Nichiren Shoshu (NE-sure-an SHOW-shu). This is one of many sects, or denominations, in Buddhism. It is one of the most popular in North America. The small group I joined became my family, my link to humanity, and the agent of changing our world.

WHO IS BUDDHA?

If you were to ask that question to a few of the 320 million people on earth today who call themselves Buddhists, some would say he is like a rabbit's foot. "He brings me good fortune."

Others would say he was the wisest man who ever lived. Still others consider him the lord of the universe, though most Buddhists do not consider him a god.

Buddha was born in a rural rice farming area that his father ruled, in northern India. Legend says his father learned from a local fortune-teller that Buddha was going to become a wise man one day, and that he would probably leave home. This meant Buddha's father would have no one to take over his kingdom after he died. So Buddha's father decided if he could surround his son with the best that money could buy, his son might stay.

Buddha, born with the name Siddhartha Gautama, was also protected from as many of the unpleasant realities of life as possible. For example, when he traveled throughout the countryside, his father ordered that all the sick and elderly should stay inside. The father didn't want his son to see these people working hard in the rice paddies.

Then one day, without warning, the young Buddha slipped out of the estate for an eye-opening tour of the kingdom. He saw things he had never seen before. He asked a servant traveling with him what was wrong with the people.

The servant pointed each person out and replied, "That person is old, the other is diseased, that man is wise, and the other is dead."

The prince became upset at all the suffering he saw as he continued to tour his father's kingdom. So he decided to do something about it. He was going to do what many other young Indian men had done: renounce all possessions and become a monk. He would live a life of self-denial. That meant leaving his home, his family, even his wife and baby son.

So he left his comfortable surroundings and his inheritance to begin training under the best teachers of his day. Like other monks, or ascetics, of his day, he probably lay on beds of nails, walked on hot coals, and starved himself in extended fasts. All this in a search for answers to the questions that plagued him.

After six years of this, he decided he was wasting his time. So he found himself a big Bo tree, sat down, and resolved not to get up until he had solved the riddles of this life. After 49 days and nights of meditation, the story goes, he reached what Buddhists call enlightenment. He finally had all the answers to life's suffering. That was how he got the name Buddha, which means "the Enlightened One."

WHAT BUDDHISTS BELIEVE

As there are many denominations in Christianity, there are many sects in Buddhism.

The more orthodox Buddhism, especially popular in Southeast Asia, is the Buddhism of the elders. It's also known as Theravada or Hinayana. These Buddhists believe that by renouncing the world and all its pleasures, and by meditation and right living, they can eliminate suffering and attain the highest goal of Buddhism, nirvana.

Nirvana is as close as these Buddhists get to our idea of heaven. Nirvana, where they believe Buddha went after he died, has been described as the transformation of a person's identity and awareness. But it's more like the extinction of self. You merge with the universe.

The *Tripitika*, an early Buddhist scripture, describes it this way:

> Nirvana is the area where there is no earth, water, fire, and air; it is not the region of infinite space, or that of infinite consciousness; it is not the region of nothing at all, nor the border between distinguishing and not distinguishing . . . It is without foundation, without continuation and without stopping. It is the end of suffering.

Because Buddhists in this sect believe selfishness is the cause of the world's problems, they practice self-denial as they journey toward enlightenment and nirvana. The monks follow about 250 commandments and the nuns 500. Women have more rules to follow, because being a woman is considered inferior to being a man. A woman, for example, must be reborn as a male before she can progress on to nirvana.

Women, in other words, are women because of bad karma. "Karma" is the Buddhist teaching that says we reap what we sow, if not in this life perhaps in the next or the next. For example, if you stole in this life, you might be reborn as an insect in the next life. That's why you will not see a can of Raid in a Buddhist's kitchen. The ant on the shelf might just be an aunt.

The goal of each person, then, is that over a period of many lifetimes they will eventually achieve that level of enlightenment Buddha reached as he sat under the tree. Only then will the cycle of reincarnation and suffering end.

A second branch of Buddhism is called Mahayana. It is popular in Vietnam, Hong Kong, Taiwan, China, Korea, Japan, and in countries to which these people have immigrated, like the United States.

Mahayana Buddhism broke off from Theravada Buddhism in the first two centuries A.D. Some scholars speculate Christians caused the break, since Mahayana Buddhism seems to merge Buddhist philosophy with some Christian doctrine. For example, some sects springing from Mahayana Buddhism worship Buddha as a god. Yet Buddha never claimed to be a god, or even a messenger sent from God. In fact, on the subject of God, Buddha was very quiet. The Amida (Pure Land) sect of Buddhism also appears to merge Buddhism with Christianity. These Buddhists believe in heaven and in the doctrine of grace that can set you free from the "wheel of suffering."

Yet, Buddhism, from its very beginning, was never based on a system of grace. Hope, for the Buddhist, came not through some gift by a compassionate god. It came through a system of works, known as the Eightfold Path.

This path to enlightenment requires Buddhists to pursue:

right knowledge, attitude, speech, action, living (occupation), effort, mindfulness (meditation), and composure. The first two deal with wisdom, the next three with conduct, and the last three with mental discipline.

For example, a Burmese monk's concept of right meditation could require him to sit in a graveyard and meditate about the decaying body parts buried beneath him. He would do this to better understand that life is temporary—an illusion at best, always changing and, therefore, not worthy of becoming attached to. How's that for following Paul's advice to think about things that are pure and lovely (Philippians 4:8)?

The Buddhism I practiced is called Nichiren Shoshu, also known as NSA (Nichiren Shoshu Academy), Sokagakkai, True Humanism, and chanting. A radical Japanese Buddhist monk called Nichiren founded it in the 13th century A.D. Today over 20 million people follow his religion in 115 countries around the world.

Buddhists from other denominations think of it as materialistic Buddhism. That's because NSA members often chant for things like jobs and new girlfriends.

What they chant is a phrase that Nichiren said was the essence of *Lotus Sutra*, a book containing what Buddhists believe are the highest teachings of Buddha. The four-word phrase chanted is: Nam-myoho-renge-kyo (nahm-ME-OH-ho-WREN-gay-KEE-OH). Literally translated, the words mean: devotion, mystic law of life and death, cause and effect, and sound or vibration. Buddhists say that by kneeling and chanting this phrase, they get into the rhythm of the universe, and good things begin to happen.

Nichiren followers would chant each day, repeating the chant one or more hours a day. I remember chanting four hours and rubbing a string of beads. I had a string with 108 large beads, representing 108 earthly desires, and 4 smaller beads, representing purity. When all the beads began to feel the same, I considered myself making progress.

I directed my chanting toward a piece of paper called the

Gohonzon, which was the object of my worship. That, of course, made it an idol. On this paper, written in Chinese, Japanese, and Sanskrit, were the names of Shinto, Hindu, and Buddhist gods we called "forces of the universe." Also on the paper was the name of the sect's founder: Nichiren.

Some people laugh when they hear I worshiped a piece of paper. But a lot of people worship paper. It's called money.

We were a militantly evangelistic group of Buddhists, always trying to win converts. If you are ever stopped on the street and asked, "Have you ever heard of Nam-myoho-renge-kyo?" you have been "shakubukued" (SHAHK-a-BOO-cooed). This is a word that means "tearing and crushing of other faiths." This is the Buddhist version of what Christians call witnessing. The small home group I was part of used to pass out thousands of slips of paper each year. The paper would include the chant, along with the time and address of an upcoming discussion meeting.

Our activity schedule was crowded. In fact, in Japan, this branch of Buddhism is called Militant Buddhism because it is so aggressive. Each week we would visit homes of new members or potential converts, to teach them how to chant or to sell them our publications. It was not unusual for the adults and young people to have discussion meetings two to five evenings a week, to talk about our physical and spiritual needs and to testify about the benefits of our religious practices.

The young people would have about two more activities a week. And for each of us, the week wouldn't have been complete without a study meeting, to review the words of our founder, whose letters have been preserved. We also studied the words of President Daisaku Ikeda, "master" of the sect. He is praised and glorified by Nichiren Shoshu devotees. His picture appears near Nichiren altars worldwide.

Then there were our annual conventions. We traveled to Seattle, Washington, D.C., New York, Los Angeles, Hawaii, and even to Japan. We put on massive cultural performances at places like Dodger Stadium, during their pregame show. Our Brass Band even dressed up as Santa Clauses and played Christmas carols for the Los Angeles mayor's Christmas party.

WHEN MY FAITH BEGAN TO SOUR

In the discussions, study sessions, and business meetings I attended, I felt free to talk about whatever was on my mind. But when I started asking questions about God and where our money was going, then I started drawing opposition.

One morning I accompanied a group of Buddhists to a meeting with NSA leaders at the World Culture Center in Santa Monica, Calif. This is the North American headquarters for NSA. There, we questioned the staff. "Where does our money go and why can't we as senior leaders look at the finances of the organization?"

All we got was a bundle of name-calling and stares. As a protest, we left the meeting en masse. Later, an inside source who happened to be a good friend of mine called me up and said, "Jim, you'd better lay low for a while."

"Why?" I asked.

"After the meeting was adjourned, I overheard two guys talking about getting their .357 Magnums and finding you guys and blowing you away."

By this time I was beginning to wonder how the compassionate Buddha fit into all this.

Why were the NSA leaders unwilling to be open about the finances?

And why did they react with similar disapproval to my questions about God? We worshiped Buddhist gods every morning, even though we called them forces of the universe.

In addition, I wondered why these divine forces didn't protect a young black girl in my group from being killed by the Freeway Strangler. Or why they didn't keep another member from hanging herself in despair.

I decided I was asking the right questions to the wrong people. So I planned a pilgrimage to Japan, where our sect was founded. All Nichiren Buddhists are encouraged to make a pilgrimage to Nichiren headquarters on Mount Fuji. There, I would raise my questions to the priests.

While I was in Japan, I had an accident in which a 200-pound sign crashed down on my back. After stays in three hospitals, I sought encouragement and advice over the phone from some Buddhist leaders I knew in Tokyo. The compassionless response was, "Go on the pilgrimage, even if you have to go in a wheelchair." But because of my injuries, I was not able to. Broken and alone, I felt the promises of Buddhism had fallen short.

HOW I BECAME A CHRISTIAN

After I returned to the United States, I continued to encounter hypocrisy in the upper leadership. Yet I made sincere attempts to work through the organizational and philosophical deficiencies. However, my attempts at gentle confrontation were met only by deceit and power maneuvers.

In a last-ditch effort, I tried to make an appointment to talk to President Daisaku Ikeda.

I contacted his office by letter and by phone—only to be denied and pushed aside. But, undaunted, I was determined to talk with him. One day I waited for him, outside his office in the Santa Monica headquarters. Eventually, I saw Ikeda head for his limousine. He walked behind a wall of Buddhist bodyguards. I got to within a few feet of him and called his name. I know he heard me, but he refused to even look my way. He got into the backseat of his car, and the driver took him away.

In that moment, I became a spiritually broken man. I felt totally lost.

Yet even after that, I was reluctant to abandon 14 years of Buddhist practice. Though I continued to speak the words of Buddhism, the vitality had left me. And I was noticing in myself more and more depravity, to the point that I could scarcely identify with a pure conscience. The leaders were not the only hypocrites. I, too, was living a lie.

The writer of Proverbs described well where I had been and where I was headed. "There is a way that seems right to a man, but in the end it leads to death" (Proverbs 16:25).

God was soon to show me the way to life. He used a Christian architect friend of mine who had gently tried witnessing to me before. She came into the blueprint store where I was working, and during our conversation I told her about my spiritual emptiness. She responded, "I've got a present for you that I'll bring by tomorrow." As she walked away, she turned to look at me behind the counter. "I've been praying for you," she said. I was deeply moved by her concern.

The next morning, there was a package waiting for me at work. It had a card on top that read, "Seek, and ye shall find; knock, and it shall be opened unto you." In the package were two books: one by J. Isamu Yamamoto called *Beyond Buddhism,* and another by Josh McDowell, *More than a Carpenter.* After reading these books, I wondered, could this be the perfect Master I have been seeking?

Soon after this, another Christian businessman learned of my spiritual confusion. He loaned me his Bible and encouraged me to read the Gospel of John. I quickly discovered that Jesus was utterly different from the Christ that Buddhist leaders told us about. I'd often heard Nichiren Shoshu leaders mockingly exclaim, "Can you believe a religion that worships a dead man on a cross?"

But here in this Book was the Living Master—the One who was not reincarnated, but resurrected; the One I had sought so desperately in men.

When I told my father about this, he introduced me to a Nazarene pastor from Santa Monica. Rev. Clarence Crites shared with me the truth of the living God. This God was not a force, as some Buddhists teach about their host of gods. This God was a Person who loved me, who created me, and who wanted me to know Him.

Clarence read to me the words of Christ Jesus: "I am the bread of life. He who comes to me will never go hungry, and he who believes in me will never be thirsty" (John 6:35). Convicted of my sin against a holy God, I laid my burden at the Savior's feet and gave Him my life. That night, my wife—a Nichiren Shoshu Buddhist for 16 years—also believed. What grace.

Nichiren, the self-proclaimed Japanese True Buddha we had followed for so many years, had said that if he found a teacher greater than himself, he would follow him. In my case, the greater Teacher found me.

6

Hinduism

AT A GLANCE

HOW IT GOT STARTED

Hinduism is the one major world religion without a single founder. It began in north India and is the product of some 5,000 years of development. Originally a religion of many gods, it eventually grew into a philosophy that focused on the idea that we are all part of the whole, like cells in a body.

KEY ATTRACTIONS

Hinduism is exotic and appears to be deeply spiritual. Reincarnation holds a special fascination for many. In addition, the hidden truths promoted by gurus attract many who are disillusioned by the dead religion of lukewarm Christianity.

WHERE IT PARTS COMPANY WITH CHRISTIANITY

Hindus worship many gods. They do not follow Jesus as the unique Son of the one eternal God. Most Hindus believe in salvation by works, through ritual offerings, chanting, or yoga. Salvation means release from the cycles of reincarnation. Many Hindus hope to become one with the universe, like a raindrop that falls into the ocean. They consider many Hindu writings as sacred.

STATUS TODAY

Hinduism is found chiefly in India, Nepal, and the Indonesian island of Bali. In the West, Hindu philosophy has been the main influence in the New Age movement. Hinduism is the world's third-largest religion, after Christianity and Islam. There are about 680 million Hindus in the world.

Mark Albrecht is a freelance writer who specializes in the study of Asian religions. He was a co-director of the Spiritual Counterfeits Project, a ministry that researches and reports on other religious groups. He is the author of Reincarnation: A Christian Appraisal (Downers Grove, Ill.: InterVarsity Press, 1982). Albrecht lives in Milwaukee.

Hinduism and the Hare Krishna:

Quest for the End of Reincarnation

By MARK ALBRECHT

HINDUISM is an old and exotic religion. You'll find in it all the bizarre trappings of dark and mysterious Asia. Nearly naked holy men meditating on mountainsides. Long-haired, bearded gurus wrapped in gold and scarlet robes. Head-shorn monks dressing stone idols.

It is an ancient philosophy of reincarnation, cosmic consciousness, repetitious chanting, and sweet incense.

When I was a college senior in southern California, I took a course in Asian religions. At first it all sounded strange and outlandish. But one day we read an old Hindu text. It spoke of mythological gods and of Hindu holy men who lived in ancient monasteries in the timeless snows of the Himalayan Mountains. It was fascinating. My imagination was captured by the lure and enchantment of the Orient.

I walked out of the classroom and looked up at the eastern horizon. It was a rare day in Los Angeles, with no smog. The late afternoon sun shone on the San Gabriel Mountain Range that encircled the city. The highest point,

Mount Baldy, was a glowing orange-pink in the fading light. On top sat a cap of snow, from a fresh winter storm. Suddenly I understood "cosmic consciousness"—our oneness with creation. I was nearly overpowered by the urge to climb Mount Baldy and sit on her peak. I wanted to contemplate the mysteries of the universe, just as Hindu monks I had been reading about had done.

I never did climb Mount Baldy, but I did think about God and His universe. Thankfully, I remained a Christian. But I have never lost my lifelong fascination with the study of Asia's religions.

Hinduism began in India, where it is still the most popular religion of the country. About 80 percent of India's population of 800 million are Hindus.

Though Hinduism began several thousand years ago, it is only a recent import to the West. As the philosophical backbone of today's New Age groups, Hinduism made a big impact on North America in the turbulent 1960s. Americans were at first amused by gurus. These were men like the small Maharishi Mahesh Yogi, who taught the old Hindu practice of transcendental meditation to the Beatles. And Swami Prabhupada, the elderly monk who founded the Hare Krishnas by hopping and chanting in New York's Greenwich Village.

However, amusement quickly turned to fascination. And by the late '60s, Westerners by the millions were sampling and embracing the ideas of Hinduism. In fact, this Hindu explosion in the West was so successful and well-orchestrated that some have called it "the Hindu countermission to the West." For it seems to have been a well-planned missionary effort organized under the guidance of the World Hindu Organization.

The spread of Hindu teachings has been remarkable. Fully 25 percent of the U.S. population now accepts Hindu and New Age ideas such as reincarnation and the belief in an impersonal God or "God-force."

HINDU TEACHINGS

Two concepts lie at the core of Hindu teachings.

Impersonal God-force. Hindu philosophers often speak of "The Absolute," a sort of universal spirit called *Brahman.*

Hindus believe that the world is really "Brahman in disguise." In other words, all matter, and especially biological and human life, are only temporary manifestations or "vibrations" coming from this universal spirit.

As a result, for many Hindus there is no difference between the creator and the creation. All things, including people, are essentially "God," even if we are unaware of this. This idea is called *pantheism,* a word that comes from the Greek *pan,* meaning "all," and *theos,* meaning "God." The word pantheism means "all is God."

This idea clashes with the Christian teaching about God. The God of Scripture is an infinite, all-powerful, loving, *personal* Creator who is distinct from and above His creation.

Reincarnation. The second basic teaching of Hinduism is reincarnation. This idea of rebirth into a new body has become popular and trendy in the last decade, especially in influential circles such as Hollywood. Shirley MacLaine often speaks of her "past lives." And Sylvester Stallone claims he once lived as a monkey in the jungles of Central America.

One reason some people are eager to accept reincarnation is it gives them an excuse for putting off moral choices. After all, we'll get another chance in the next life.

The doctrine of reincarnation says all forms of life are somehow reborn after death. For humans, this means we are reborn into a better status if we have behaved well. On the other hand, if we have lived a bad life, we can be reborn as a person who pays for his previous sins by experiencing suffering and poverty. (For the Hindu, these past sins are called *karma.*)

Reincarnation does not mesh with the central Christian teaching of resurrection. Christians believe that each believer rises after death to an eternal life in heaven.

LIVING THE HINDU RELIGION

Religious practice takes many forms in Hinduism. These forms are often colorful and bizarre. The holy city of Rishikesh in north India sits beside the Ganges River, nestled among the foothills of the Himalayan Mountains. If you walk a mile upstream from the town, as I have, you can see the strange and varied faces of Hinduism.

Naked holy men, known as ascetics, paint their bodies with bright colors and sit on rocks in the middle of the river. They will meditate for hours, sometimes for days. Monasteries line the riverbank. These sacred houses are filled with novice disciples who wander about with orange robes and shaved heads. Enlightened spiritual teachers called gurus preside over the monasteries. Other gurus live in caves or huts in the hills, where they perform meditation and yoga for years, in an attempt to attain salvation.

As you walk past small temples in the hills and along the river, you can hear chanting and chimes, and smell the sweet aroma of incense. Inside the temples there is an eerie half-light. Scores of stone and wooden idols peer down at worshipers through the smoky haze of flickering candles.

The sights, sounds, and smells I encountered at Rishikesh illustrate the religious practices of the devout Hindu. The many gods I saw in the temples are the means people use to focus on the Absolute, or Brahman. There are literally millions of gods in Hinduism, and people worship them in a simple ceremony called *puja*. There, the devout offer the god flowers, food, incense, and prayer.

Gurus. For the Hindu, his guru is more than just a pastor or priest. The guru is a man who has supposedly attained enlightenment after thousands of reincarnations. Some gurus are even worshiped as divine figures, more powerful than the gods. Gurus usually demand complete obedience from their disciples. The disciples dutifully live spartan lives, enduring long hours of manual labor, meditation, and little sleep.

I once got a chance to see one of the world's master gurus

in action. His name was Swami Muktananda. He was a small man who usually dressed in an orange robe and wore a knitted cap over his bald head. Before his death in 1982, Muktananda had a following of several hundred thousand disciples in over 100 centers around the world. He popularized the Hindu slogan "Worship your own inner self. God dwells within you as you."

It was 1980 when I saw him. I sat down with a large audience in his temple in Oakland, Calif. The Swami sat on a stage, perched on a large pillow. He looked out toward the mass of disciples and seekers who were sitting on the hard floor. One by one his disciples came forward with gifts: expensive jewelry, art, keys to their autos. A few brought bottles of liquor or cartons of cigarettes, which symbolized the vices they wished to rid themselves of.

Muktananda received each gift, then touched the giver with a long peacock feather. This was to transfer some of his spiritual power to them. The idea is a bit like jump-starting a dead battery. You transfer energy from a charged battery to a dead one. Some of the people actually fell to the floor and had to be carried off.

This act is an initiation into the guru's spiritual family. It is called *shaktipat* (SHOCK-tee-pot). It creates a psychological and spiritual bond between the guru and the disciple. It is actually a form of spiritual bondage that bears some resemblance to demonic possession. The very will of the disciple is taken over by the guru.

Meditation. This is another key element in Hinduism. Hindus do not pray the way Christians do. Instead, they meditate by repeating a word or phrase over and over for hours each day. This has a mood-altering effect on the brain, similar to taking drugs. Many techniques of meditation have evolved over thousands of years. Some are quite powerful and effective. Regular meditation actually makes a person "high," producing a kind of religious experience that seems to confirm the teachings of Hinduism.

Self-salvation. This is the single goal of all the religious activity by Hindus. Most Hindus do not believe, as Christians do, that people are saved by the grace and love of God. Salvation is something a person must earn through many lifetimes of devotion, yoga, meditation, and other disciplines.

Even their concept of salvation is considerably different from the Christian understanding of being saved and going to heaven. The Hindu seeks to burn off all the soul's sins, or karma. This process is a long and painful journey that usually takes thousands of lifetimes of suffering. Actually, existence itself is thought of as suffering. So, salvation for many Hindus is not continued existence in heaven, but *the end of personal existence.*

Gurus explain this by saying that final liberation is like a drop of water falling into the ocean. The drop ceases to have any kind of separate existence. It simply becomes one with the ocean. In this analogy, the individual soul merges with the universe, or the Absolute. Final salvation in Hinduism closely resembles extinction, not unlike the atheist's concept of death.

A CASE STUDY: HARE KRISHNAS

On a warm September afternoon in 1965, a thin, bald, 70-year-old Indian man dressed in an orange robe walked into the middle of a park in New York City. He began to dance and chant.

Accompanying himself with cymbals, he repeated a 16-word mantra over and over:

> "Hare Krishna, Hare Krishna,
> Krishna Krishna, Hare Hare.
> Hare Rama, Hare Rama,
> Rama Rama, Hare Hare."

Curious people began to stand around and listen. After several hours of this, the old man opened up the Hindu scripture known as the *Bhagavad Gita* and preached a sermon. The message always concluded with his version of a "gospel presentation." He explained that by chanting the name of the lord Krishna, the highest of the Hindu gods, a person could discover the meaning of life and attain enlightenment.

The man was known as His Divine Grace A. C. Bhaktivedanta Swami Prabhupada (PRAH-boo-PAY-duh). He founded the Hare Krishna organization in the West. By the time he died in 1977, Swami Prabhupada had a worldwide following of tens of thousands in over 300 centers, was chauffeured about in black limousines, and presided over a multi-million-dollar organization known as the International Society for Krishna Consciousness (ISKCON).

ISKCON is an interesting case study. It is one of the most widely known Hindu movements to take root and grow in the Western world. It also presents a challenge to the Christian church, since Krishna devotees are dedicated disciples, living self-sacrificial lives of complete devotion to their religion.

The Hare Krishnas are just one of many sects in Hinduism. By the 16th century (about the time of the Protestant Reformation in Europe) Hinduism had split into two branches. The traditional old Hinduism thought of God or Brahman as impersonal. But most people found it difficult to relate to such an impersonal force.

As a result, a growing number of Hindu thinkers began to emphasize the personal side of the Absolute, focusing on the god Krishna, the hero of the *Bhagavad Gita.* According to the teachings of this school, a person could achieve a sort of personal relationship, or divine communion with Krishna through the systematic chanting of his name.

Because of this, some say Krishna is similar to Christ. But there are far more differences than similarities.

Krishna is not a historical figure, and the *Bhagavad Gita* is a fictional epic. Krishna did not die for the sins of the world. And devotion to Krishna does not involve creative, interactive prayer. The "relationship" with Krishna is sustained by chanting the 16-word mantra over 1,000 times each day. Krishna's devotees must earn their salvation.

Whether or not one agrees with their beliefs, the devotion of the Hare Krishnas to their religion is quite remarkable. Members leave behind all their earthly possessions, often giving them to ISKCON. They then take up life in a local temple. The men shave their heads, and everyone dresses in loose Indian clothing. Life is carefully regimented, to the point that personal decisions and choices become unnecessary; the temple leadership decides who does what and when. Everyone rises at 3 A.M. for a cold shower and some early chanting. The idols in the temple are then dressed for the day and fed by setting food offerings in front of them.

Krishna disciples spend a large part of the day raising funds and trying to win converts by selling ISKCON books and magazines at airports or malls. The disciples also chant and dance in public. They spend their evenings with more chanting, interspersed with idol worship. At 9 P.M. they retire to a thin mat on the hard floor.

ISKCON members are strict vegetarians. They are also forbidden to use coffee, tobacco, or alcohol. In addition, they are discouraged from reading outside materials such as magazines or newspapers, and they are told to keep their personal conversation related to Krishna. Contact with old friends and family is also kept to a minimum. These social dynamics are typical of the mind control practiced by many cults. Added to this control is the constant daily chanting, which has a hypnotic and sedative effect on the mind. This tends to keep the members in line.

Whatever we may think of the Hare Krishnas and their teachings, we must admit that North American Christians today would be hard pressed to measure up to ISKCON's discipline, obedience, and willingness to engage in evangelism. Generally speaking, Hinduism tends to be much better at integrating religion into all areas of life. In India I do not find so much of a division between religious life and secular life. In the West, the church has been compromised by a culture that has raised artificial divisions between religion and "nonspiritual" activities such as work.

Yet, in the final analysis Hinduism is a classic example of a *human* religion. It is oriented toward self-salvation, or works. The love and grace of God matter little.

I saw this clearly one day when I was climbing through Himalayan foothills in north India. I came upon a holy man sitting in a small cave. Despite the chill temperatures, he was dressed only in a thin loincloth. His face was painted with Hindu symbols, and on his forehead were the three horizontal white stripes that signified his devotion to the god Shiva. His long, matted hair and beard framed his penetrating dark eyes.

"Why are you doing this?" I asked.

He smiled only slightly as he replied in excellent English: "You may not understand. I was born to a wealthy family in Bombay and have a university degree. At the age of 30 I realized it was all meaningless."

He went on to explain that this was his 1,742nd lifetime. He said that being born again on the wheel of reincarnation would mean only more suffering, no matter what his status in life. So he decided to earn his salvation by renouncing all and living as an ascetic.

"This means I meditate eight hours each day and eat only roots, berries, wild grains, and plants," he said. "I drink from the holy River Ganges which runs below. When I die, I shall not reincarnate and return to this planet of suffering and woe. I have attained enlightenment."

Despite all that is good and noble in Hinduism, it fails to offer real hope in the battle against evil. The cycle of reincarnation and suffering, with its chaos and injustice, seems to have no end. As people attain enlightenment and are absorbed into the universe, they are replaced by new souls that are full of ignorance.

Ultimately, there is no redemption in Hinduism because there is no recognition of Jesus as the Lamb of God who takes away the sin of the world.

Unity

AT A GLANCE

HOW IT GOT STARTED

Charles and Myrtle Fillmore started Unity School of Christianity in 1889. It began after Myrtle said she was healed of tuberculosis, after repeating a mind-over-matter phrase she heard in a lecture: "I am a child of God, and therefore I do not inherit sickness." Two years later, she said, the symptoms were gone.

KEY ATTRACTIONS

Unity is a power-of-positive-thinking religion that doesn't preach hellfire and damnation. It teaches everyone will be saved, and through mind power we can control our health, finances, and future.

WHERE IT PARTS COMPANY WITH CHRISTIANITY

Unity says there is no literal heaven or hell, there is no Satan, and Jesus was no more divine than humans are. Jesus was just a man who became aware of His divinity, as humans can do. Most members of Unity believe reaching this level of awareness takes many lifetimes, through reincarnation.

STATUS TODAY

Unity has about 200,000 members and is growing, especially on the east and west coasts.[1] On an average Sunday, 104,000 worship in 574 churches and 245 smaller satellite ministries, primarily in the United States. Annual subscriptions to Unity magazines, including *Wee Wisdom*, has hit 3 million.

Stephen Miller is an editor and writer for the Church of the Nazarene Headquarters, Kansas City. In researching for this chapter, Miller interviewed Unity leaders, visited their churches and headquarters, and read their literature. He edits the Dialog Series of books and Illustrated Bible Life *magazine.*

Unity School of Christianity:
Mind Power

By STEPHEN M. MILLER

I BROKE OUT in a cold and clammy sweat during the first Unity worship service I attended.

It's because I'm not a toucher. I don't even put my arm around my wife when I settle in to listen to the sermon in my home church. But the morning I stepped into the 1,000-seat auditorium of Unity Village Chapel at Unity headquarters near Kansas City, I realized I had been engulfed by a swarm of huggers, kissers, and hand-holders.

I didn't start sweating until the end of the service. Since no one knew me, I thought I'd be able to escape with nothing more intimate than a handshake. I was wrong. Most Unity churches, this one included, close each service by having everyone stand, hold hands, and sing "The Peace Song" ("Let there be peace on earth, / And let it begin with me. . . .")

It was Father's Day, but I visited the church alone. My wife and children were at our church, while I researched Unity by attending its two morning services. Sitting to my right was a young woman who had slipped in late. To my left

63

was the aisle. That meant at hand-holding time I had to stand in the middle of the aisle, reach out to a second woman, and link the two sections of the auditorium together.

As I stood in the aisle, fumbled through the unfamiliar song from the '50s, and held the hands of two women I didn't know from Eve, my pores started to pump out a chilling sweat.

Then everybody started to sway. Left and right, to the rhythm of the music. I'm not a swayer. When I was in elementary school, Mom had our preacher write a note to my gym teacher so I wouldn't have to square dance.

With the last phrase of the song, everyone raised their held hands over their heads. Mine got lifted too. And with the last note came the hand squeezes. I got one for each hand. I can't remember if I gave any in reflex.

I was so unnerved by all this, I nearly decided to leave and skip the second service, which featured a different speaker. But I convinced myself to stay.

Since that first service, I've visited others, listened to tapes of still others, and interviewed Unity preachers, professors, and administrators. These are pleasant, upbeat people. Even Norman Vincent Peale said so. This author of *Power of Positive Thinking* and publisher of *Guideposts* magazine confirmed for me that in one of his visits to the Chapel, he complimented the congregation by saying, "Unity must be a good faith, for the Unity people I have known have been very good people."

Yet, Unity lives on the fringe of Christianity. Some critics say beyond the fringe, over the edge, and off the wall.

Joseph Wolpert, who teaches history at Unity's ministerial school, told me that the most unfair criticism people make of Unity is they call it a cult. "People who say Unity is a cult are more cultlike than Unity is. [In Unity] people have the freedom to be themselves because we're not imposing a whole bunch of stuff they have to believe."

NO CREED, NO MANUAL

In my denomination, we have 16 "Articles of Faith" that describe what we believe. One such article says, "We believe in Jesus Christ, the Second Person of the Triune Godhead."

Unity has no such creed. At least none in writing. Yet there are two prevailing teachings. And if this 100-year-old religious movement that's still evolving into a denomination ever does draft some articles of faith, these two will sit at the top of the list.

1. There is only one power in the universe. This power is God, and it is good.

Most Unity folks don't believe in Satan and his army of demons. But neither do 31 percent of American Protestants, according to a 1990 Gallup poll.[2]

How ironic that Charles Fillmore chose as Unity's symbol a winged disk from ancient Egypt. You'll see the symbol in nearly every Unity church. And you'll see it in their publications. Fillmore said that when he first saw the Egyptian symbol, "I felt that I had had something to do with it in a previous incarnation [life]."[3]

Frank Giudici, who teaches the Bible at Unity's ministerial school, says that what they call the winged globe symbolizes the freedom of the soul. A Unity video says it represents the earth being lifted in consciousness. *Unity* magazine said it represents the soul giving wings to the body.

I called an Egyptologist for his opinion. Frank Yurco, who lectures at the University of Chicago, said it represents a fear of demons and evil gods.

"It's not a globe," Yurco said. "It's a disk. It represents the sun-god." The wings show that the sun-god, Re, flies across the sky.

Egyptians painted this symbol above the doorway to temples. They believed Re could keep evil gods away. In fact, Egyptian art that shows the sun setting into the underworld also often shows the demons fleeing. For as the light of Re displaced darkness, the Egyptians believed, the good of Re displaced evil.

2. Thoughts held in our minds show up in our lives.

Even John Wesley, Methodist founder, taught that our thoughts can affect our health. "Why," he asked in his 1759 journal, "do not all physicians consider how bodily disorders are caused or influenced by the mind?" Unity goes further.

Christopher Chenoweth, pastor of Unity Village Chapel, told his congregation what he did when he felt sick one Saturday.

"I was so sick I didn't think I'd be able to stand up on Sunday morning," he said. So he began repeating an affirmation. That's Unity's version of prayer. Unity people don't usually say prayers like, "Lord, help me get well." That assumes God is "up there somewhere." And it assumes God may not want you well. Unity people believe they are a part of God, and He always wants them well.

The affirmation Chenoweth repeated throughout the day was: "Every hand that touches me is the healing hand of Jesus Christ. God is healing me now."

"I said that affirmation Saturday afternoon 150 times, to the point that I forgot about the affirmation. And then the cleaning lady came in and shook my hand for the raise I gave her. At that moment there was a jolt that went through my body, and I was better."

Frank Giudici says he teaches his ministerial students that everything that happens to us springs from our mind. "God gave us control of our lives," he said.

People are responsible for their own sickness, poverty, and damaged relationships. I asked Giudici what this would mean to 200 people on a jetliner whose engines had quit, leaving the plane plummeting to the earth.

"God's given us the freedom to turn the engines on or not to," he said.

"But," I replied, "if those engines don't come back on, you leave your people guilty."

"No," he said. "They make the choice to feel guilty." Of course, that's assuming they survive.

A friend of mine, Ann, told me this prevailing sense of guilt is one of the reasons she left Unity. She said she grew weary of being told that every bad thing that happened to her was her fault. "I got tired of people telling me that the reason certain things weren't working well for me is that I hadn't forgiven someone enough or I hadn't said the right affirmation."

SO, CALL ME A HERETIC

Unity people admit they are heretics, as far as orthodox Christianity is concerned. They say they teach what Jesus taught, before church councils started getting together to define *orthodox* by drafting things like the Apostles' Creed and theologies about original sin, the Trinity, and Judgment Day.

"We're Gnostic," Frank Giudici told me. Gnosticism was a second-century teaching church councils later judged as heresy. "The Gnostic says you're saved through knowledge," Giudici said. "Well, Unity teaches that. We're Gnostic in that we believe you're saved when you understand that the Christ indwells you."

Unity teaches that Christ is in everyone, so everyone will be saved. Saved from what? Not sin. And certainly not hell. Unity people don't believe in hell. "Your own false thinking, that's the only thing to be saved from," Giudici explained.

Because Unity doesn't have a written creed, I can't tell you what Unity believes about key subjects in Christianity. All I can do is quote Unity leaders, who sometimes disagree with each other. Here's a sampling of what I've learned from them.

God. "God never says no," Giudici told me. "God can't say anything but yes."

I argued that sometimes "No" is the loving response. Such as, "No, you don't want to play on the railroad track."

Giudici said God would respond by saying, "OK, if you want that, you can have it. However, remember there's something better. But if you insist on this, you can have it."

Joseph Wolpert, a colleague of Giudici's who also teaches future Unity ministers, presents God differently. The Father's Day I sweat through my first Unity hand-holding, Wolpert was the guest speaker. He admits to having an evangelical streak in him, saying he met Jesus in a personal religious experience. That sets him apart from most Unity people I've talked with. Wolpert gently chastised the congregation.

He said some Unity folks treat God backward. "God spelled backward is dog," he told them. "You say, 'God, I need a job. Here's an affirmation. Fetch.'"

Jesus. Critics of Unity say the people don't believe in the divinity of Jesus. Don Jennings, pastor of the Unity church in Omaha, says otherwise. He visited the Chapel one Sunday and told the congregation and radio audience, "We believe in the divinity of Jesus Christ, totally, completely." Then he added, "We believe in the divinity of you, every one of you."

I called him later and asked what the difference was between us and Jesus. He said, "Jesus did and we haven't." Jesus was a man who became aware of the divinity within Him. He reached oneness with God, as each of us can.

Unity founder Charles Fillmore said Jesus did this over many lifetimes, and that in previous lives Jesus had been Moses, Elisha, and David. These lifetimes were His "schools." Eventually, Jesus raised His consciousness to the point of reaching oneness with God and achieving a glorified body.

Frank Giudici told me, "I believe that Jesus totally spiritualized His body. How? By spiritualizing His thoughts."

For us, as it was for Jesus, according to Giudici, "It's a process of evolution. One of these days, I believe, we will levitate. We don't do it now because we don't have the consciousness for it," he said, "because we're too dense up here." He pointed to his head.

The Bible. In Unity, the Bible isn't the final, authoritative Word of God that it is for evangelicals.

Unity preachers and teachers I've talked with put equal

weight on insights from other religious books and from their own quiet times of meditation.

Giudici told me, "God is speaking to me like God was speaking to Paul."

Rev. Jennings said, in a radio broadcast, "Only half of the Bible is between pages. The other half is within your own mind."

Unity has a special fondness for the teachings of Jesus and holds them in higher esteem than the teachings of others in the Bible. In the same broadcast, Jennings said, "Paul was certainly inspired in much of what he said. [Yet] sometimes we have to kind of sort through and sift out what was Paul and what was Christ speaking through Paul."

Though Unity folks hold the teachings of Jesus above those of the apostles, Unity people feel free to reinterpret even Jesus, if His teachings don't seem to make sense.

Take John 3:16. Or as comedian Henny Youngman might put it, "Take John 3:16, please."

"For God so loved the world that he gave his one and only Son, that whoever believes in him shall not perish but have eternal life."

Most Unity people I talked with don't believe Jesus is the only Son of God. They don't believe we have to profess Christ as Lord to be saved. They don't believe anyone will perish. And they don't believe eternal life is something we can attain through the forgiveness of sins. So Unity does not take John 3:16 literally.

Giudici gave me his interpretation of the verse. "I'm not saying this is what the Bible says," he explained. "But I am free to interpret according to the way I think God is leading me to interpret."

Giudici's interpretation: "For God so loved the world that he/she individualized himself/herself in you and in me. Not so that we may gain eternal life, but so that we may enjoy more abundantly the eternal life that we already have."

Reincarnation. This is one of the distinctive teachings of

Unity. Most members believe they'll keep coming back to earth as humans until they reach the oneness with God they say Jesus achieved, as He proved by overcoming death.

Giudici said you can't support reincarnation from Scripture. But he says the teaching helps explain some evil in the world, like why some babies are born blind. The theory is that the infant made some bad decisions in a previous life.

It also helps explain geniuses. Rev. Jennings gave me a hypothetical example, "Maybe 100 years from now I might grow up to be a great orator, because for the last seven lifetimes I've been practicing."

Jennings said that after each life, he believes people lose their identity. "What would go on is not my personality. What would go on would be that unit of energy that has learned everything up to this point."

Unity can even get a bit sci-fi on this subject.

Giudici said, "I believe in the possibility that we can incarnate on another planet, in another form."

Heaven and hell. Unity preachers say people need to raise their consciousness and strive for oneness with God. But there's not a lot of talk about what happens when we reach this goal.

Rev. Jennings told me that when people reach total oneness with God, they no longer need a body. "I think they would be assimilated back into the cosmos and would cease to exist as a separate identity. I don't teach that a lot, because people don't want to hear it."

Others in Unity disagree with Jennings. Wolpert, the history prof with an evangelical streak, said, "I believe we continue in some type of a living arrangement."

One thing Unity people agree on is that all roads eventually lead to God. So Unity respects other religions.

Rev. Chenoweth told his congregation, "Religions are like spokes on a wheel that lead to the one God."

Jennings told me, "It is great if you find [in Unity] what complements your life-style and what it is you're seeking out of life." And he added, "If it doesn't, then we want to help you find the church that will. And if it's a Southern Baptist church or a Jewish synagogue or an Islam mosque, I don't care. Just find God somewhere and hang on."

Even evangelically tainted Wolpert agrees. I asked him how all this could possibly mesh with Jesus' words in John 14:6, "I am the way and the truth and the life. No one comes to the Father except through me."

Wolpert asked if Jesus is the Word, God incarnate, "Why is it not possible that the same Word incarnated [came to earth] in a Hindu form or in a Buddhist form?"

But would God point humans in one spiritual direction in one lifetime, and in an opposite direction in another incarnation? There are a lot of differences between Christianity and Hinduism.

I asked Wolpert why Unity folks don't believe they will be punished in the afterlife for sins they committed in this life. I cited Luke 12:5, "But I will show you whom you should fear: Fear him who, after the killing of the body, has power to throw you into hell."

He said, "Everybody takes [out of scripture] what they're comfortable with and just ignores what they're not. So that's not a piece of scripture Unity people would even take more than two glances at."

UNITY TOMORROW

Unity has resisted calling itself a denomination. It began as a religious movement to "make Baptists better Baptists and Catholics better Catholics," as they still often say.

Unity started by printing materials and creating a prayer ministry in which they prayed about requests that were sent in. But the Fillmores encouraged people to stay in their own religion.

Later, the Fillmores began holding worship services on Sundays, and Unity churches began to spring up. At the moment, there are no written rules a person has to agree to abide by to join Unity.

I asked Rev. Jennings if he thought the rules would come, eventually. He said religious movements "either die out, or they become a denomination and get real structured." In fact, my own denomination grew out of the 19th-century holiness movement.

For Unity, the structures are forming. The Association of Unity Churches directs the work of the churches. Its offices are on the 1,400-acre Unity headquarters. Though Unity has no creed, association Director Glenn Mosley said he is trying to figure ways to keep Unity preachers from going too far overboard in their teachings. In a rare move, the association recently expelled a church that refused to quit teaching that crystals have power to heal.

Other yet unwritten no-no's are astrology, palm reading, and channeling. The association's current strategy for keeping these New Age teachings out of their churches is to refuse to ordain ministers who approve of these practices.

The broader organization, Unity School of Christianity, is headed by Connie Fillmore, a great-granddaughter of Charles and Myrtle. She has no direct control over the churches but runs nearly everything else, from the publishing, to the ministerial training, to the 24-hour Silent Unity prayer ministry that generates most of the movement's nearly $30 million annual income. (With answers to prayer come what Fillmore calls "love offerings.")

I asked Fillmore, who is unmarried and 43, how she was selected president of Unity. Her father held the position until he stepped down into the role of chairman of the board of trustees in 1987. That's when his daughter became president. Connie Fillmore's staff repeatedly told me the president doesn't grant interviews. (The religion editor for the *Kansas City Star* told me she has not been able to get an interview, either.) But Fillmore agreed to respond in writing to questions I submitted in writing.

She said Unity's leadership has been "at the choice and according to the talents of the family members." Connie Fillmore has a bachelor's degree in psychology. She was ordained in 1976, after completing Unity's two-year ministerial training. Her résumé also says she's a graduate of the American Management Association's Executive Effectiveness Course. I called AMA. They do have the course. It takes two weeks to complete.

Fillmore said, "My tenure as president is indefinite. It is my job, and I assume I will continue to hold it as long as I am performing my duties in a satisfactory manner and I choose to continue."

In spite of Unity's unusual management arrangement and unorthodox theology, the gap between Unity and orthodox Christianity is slowly closing.

Unity is worshiping in the church setting. Some of their preachers are even serving Communion and wearing crosses around their necks. Joseph Wolpert wears a cross. And this, in a movement that has shied away from focusing on any kind of suffering. Even the suffering of Jesus.

When I asked Rev. Chenoweth why he didn't use the cross, as others are beginning to do, he said, "If Jesus had died today, He would have probably been sent to the electric chair, and there would be little electric chairs we would be hanging around our necks."

Wolpert says he wears the cross as a symbol of the Resurrection and eternal life. That's why Jesus died, Wolpert said. Not to save us from our sins, but to prove there is eternal life.

As Unity takes steps toward orthodox Christianity, some orthodox Christians are taking steps toward Unity. Norman Vincent Peale and Robert Schuller are both well-known for their upbeat messages that downplay sin and suffering.

Even in evangelical churches across the country, there has been a trend in recent years toward focusing on how to improve our quality of life, spiritual and otherwise. This trend has moved away from focusing on the underlying problem of unconfessed sin and God's judgment against sin.

Prosperity preachers contribute to the closing gap, even though many argue these preachers are anything but orthodox. At least they present themselves as orthodox, so they end up blurring the lines of distinction between Unity and orthodox Christianity.

Men like Kenneth Hagin, Robert Tilton, and Kenneth Copeland are so close to Unity teaching that it has Frank Giudici downright excited. As I met with Giudici in his office and asked him about this, he jumped up and grabbed a photocopy of an article in *Time* magazine. The article, "Heresy on the Airwaves," reviewed a book that attacks televangelists.[4]

It quotes Hagin: "You are as much an incarnation [of God] as is Jesus of Nazareth." It says Hagin maintains that even Jesus had to get born again.

It quotes Tilton: "That's right! You can actually tell God what you would like His part in the covenant to be!" Tilton's plan begins, "Step One: Let God Know What You Need from Him. New Car. New Job. Fitness. House. Finances. Salvation."

Giudici told me he's passing out copies of the article in his classes. And what does he tell the students about it?

"Look, folks, they're catching up."

1. Statistics describing Unity are from Unity School of Christianity headquarters.

2. George Gallup, Jr., *Kansas City Star,* August 25, 1990, E-11.

3. James Dillet Freeman, *The Story of Unity* (Unity Village, Mo.: Unity Books, 1954), 67.

4. March 5, 1990, 62.

8

New Age

AT A GLANCE

HOW IT STARTED

The roots run at least as deep as the 1960s. That's when many people became disappointed with traditional Christianity, and when they began experimenting with Eastern religions. Actress Shirley MacLaine popularized New Age beliefs. She did this with her miniseries "Out on a Limb," along with books, seminars, and videos.

KEY ATTRACTIONS

New Age promises people they can be in total control of their life. People have the unlimited power of God within—power to achieve success, health, and happiness.

WHERE IT PARTS COMPANY WITH CHRISTIANITY

It emphasizes the supernatural, such as consulting the dead and using crystals for healing. It teaches reincarnation, that God is a Force instead of a Person, and there is no need to repent of sin.

STATUS TODAY

There is no organizational structure or headquarters, just millions of people around the world being influenced by New Age teachings. MacLaine's three books alone, *Out on a Limb, Dancing in the Light,* and *Going Within,* have sold over 6 million copies.

Douglas Groothuis is author of several books about the New Age, including Confronting the New Age *and* Revealing the New Age Jesus **(both by InterVarsity). He is a campus minister at the University of Oregon and lives in Eugene.**

New Age:

The Impersonal God Within

BY DOUGLAS GROOTHUIS

THE COMPACT DISC looked innocent enough. It was a "Christmas collection" of instrumental pieces arranged and performed by contemporary musicians. Each song was a soft and mellow variation on a traditional Christmas melody. But something was wrong.

The accompanying booklet gives the performers' thoughts about how their music relates to Christmas. One pianist, David Lanz, had this to say: "As people rush to create the effect of Christmas, we sometimes cloud, or lose, its very spirit." Most Christians would heartily agree, so far. But there is more: "That essence is the symbolic rebirth of the Christ in mankind."

What does that mean?

Lanz, one of many New Age musicians, uses the Christian *vocabulary*, but he has redefined the words. When he says, "The Christ," he does not mean Jesus, as the one and only Christ. He means a Positive Energy or a Force we can tap into, like "the Force" in *Star Wars.*

And when he speaks of the "rebirth of the Christ in mankind," he refers to an awakening to the power he believes is inside all of us. We are reborn, New Agers say, not by faith in a *Person,* Jesus the Christ. We are reborn by realizing that a *Power* within is simply awaiting our discovery. Lanz and others see this self-discovery as the key to ushering in a New Age of peace and happiness.

This is far from the essence of Christmas. But it is the essence of the New Age movement. What could be more deceptive than a "Christmas collection" that denies Christ and promotes the New Age movement?

New Age music is only one small segment of a growing social movement that is leaving its mark on all aspects of society, including education, business, medicine, and politics.

WHAT IS THE NEW AGE MOVEMENT?

The New Age movement springs from the ancient teachings of Eastern mystics and from other pagan religions. These beliefs became popular in America during the social and spiritual upheaval of the 1960s.

People disenchanted with stale Christianity began picking up some of these beliefs and merging them with their own. What they ended up with is a set of beliefs about God, humanity, and salvation that are counterfeits of biblical truth.

God within. New Agers, unlike secular humanists, believe in God. Yet their God is not the personal and moral Being we find in the Bible. God is, instead, an impersonal Force or Principle in all things.

New Agers believe there is no division between Creator and creation. All is one, and this mystical Oneness is God. But God is an It, not a He. New Agers believe everything is God, especially themselves. Humans are in essence divine, although most have somehow forgotten or neglected their divinity.

Rediscovering and releasing this divinity is the goal they say we should seek.

In the television miniseries and book *Out on a Limb*, actress Shirley MacLaine told about her conversion to New Age thinking. She said she talked with New Agers, read occult books, and consulted the dead through channels, or mediums. She even said she had an out-of-body experience while relaxing in a hot-springs bath.

At one point in the movie, she was standing on a beach

and yelling, with arms outstretched, "I am God, I am God, I am God!" For Christians, this is blasphemy. For New Agers, it is enlightenment.

Conversion. The Bible teaches that conversion comes through repentance and faith in Jesus as Lord and Savior. The New Age says this is incorrect.

Conversion, New Age says, has nothing to do with confessing sin or living a holy life. Conversion is enlightenment. That means wakening up to a Power already in us. This is what New Age musician David Lanz called the "rebirth of the Christ in mankind."

New Agers say Jesus was a New Ager. He was a spiritually aware person who discovered the Christ power within himself, as we can. So He is an example of what we, too, can attain. But He is not uniquely Lord. And we do not turn to Him for conversion. Instead, we look to Him as a spiritual model.

New Age transformation or conversion comes only after we turn off our rational minds and open up to the Power within through meditation, yoga, visualization, hypnosis, trances, or other Eastern mystical techniques.

There are many roads to conversion, New Agers say, such as transcendental meditation. Meditators focus on an assigned Hindu holy word or mantra, which they repeat hundreds of times. Eventually, TM teachers say, the meditator stops thinking and begins to discover the source of Creative Intelligence (God) within.

Psychic powers. Once people have discovered their divine essence through meditation, yoga, or some other mind-altering experience, they can begin to tap into supernatural powers.

New Agers call this the paranormal. They say it's a power not available to those who function on the lower level of consciousness.

Many who practice Eastern meditation claim to experience psychic phenomena such as predicting the future, reading others' minds, and moving objects through mind power alone.

If we are actually God, New Agers argue, why shouldn't we expect to experience these extraordinary events? God, after all, has no limits.

Since this "higher dimension" is open to us, we are free to contact unearthly beings who have tapped into their potential and who want to communicate with us. Channelers contact these entities and serve as mouthpieces for their messages.

Common themes that come from these supposedly advanced spirit beings are that we are all God, we do not sin, we have unlimited potential, there is no literal heaven or hell, and we are entering a New Age of peace and happiness in the world. The beings often have biblical names like Jonah.

Reincarnation. Instead of teaching that we have only one life in which we submit to God, the New Age insists it may take many lifetimes to fully release our divine powers. Death is not the doorway to eternal life or eternal death. It simply marks the migration of the soul from one body to another.

One woman I spoke with called herself a "New Age Christian." She told me Jesus himself taught reincarnation.

"You see," she explained, "Jesus said John the Baptist was Elijah, the prophet. So John must have been the reincarnation of Elijah."

I told her Jesus was using a figure of speech that was not meant to be taken literally. She then accused me of not taking the Bible literally. But I went on to say that Jesus meant John had a ministry like Elijah's. Besides, I said, Jesus could not have been a reincarnated Elijah because Elijah never died. The prophet went directly to heaven on a chariot of fire. In addition, John denied being the literal Elijah (John 1:21).

People like this woman have no fear of facing a holy and

just God at death. They think they can come back and have another try at life.

Reincarnation also appeals to people fascinated by the idea of having lived previous lives. Some go to hypnotists who supposedly "regress" them to earlier incarnations— which are often famous and fascinating people like Napoleon, Cleopatra, or even Jesus himself.

THE APPEAL

The New Age movement attracts many because it is so positive.

In health care, it claims to treat the "whole person" and help people open up to spiritual avenues of healing not recognized by traditional medicine. For example, MacLaine advises that people with cancer of the abdomen be placed in a yellow room, because yellow is the color "frequency" of that part of the body. And in one of the "Higher Self" seminars she conducted in the late '80s, she told the audience to think about someone who had hurt them. Have a conversation with that person, MacLaine said. One woman told a reporter, "I saw my father there, who died three months ago." Another said, "I talked to my mother. I thanked her for the lessons she gave me in the past, and I forgave her for our conflicts."

In education, New Age teaches children to lie motionless and visualize their bodies filled with light. This is supposed to allow them to tap into a universal mind, through "inner helpers" or "guides" who lead them into adventures and stimulate their imagination. Children also learn yoga, a Hindu discipline, as a part of physical education classes.

In the business world, New Age seminars such as one called "the Forum" tell participants that if they get in touch with their inner being, they can totally control their circumstances and unleash their limitless potential. (The man who started the Forum has now sold it, after claims by family and former employees of incest, rape, and spouse abuse.)

CLASH WITH CHRISTIANITY

What does the Bible say about New Age beliefs?

1. From Genesis to Revelation, the Bible says God is a personal and moral Being. He is not the impersonal Principle or Power of New Age confusion. He is the Creator of the universe and the Moral Lawgiver for all humanity.

This personal God tells Moses that His name is "I am who I am" (Exodus 3:14), not "It is what it is."

God creates, knows, commands, and judges. He also sends His only Son into the world. These are the actions of a personal Being, not an impersonal Force.

2. Humans are not gods in disguise, but creatures of the Creator. We are like God in that we are made in His image (Genesis 1:26-28). But this means that we, like God, are persons. We are far short of being gods. Although we are more like God than anything else in the physical universe (see Psalm 8), we fall pitifully short of His power and holiness. To aspire to godhood is the height of arrogance.

In claiming divinity, people have fallen into the same trap Satan has used since the beginning. The serpent tempted Adam and Eve by promising them that if they disobeyed God, they would be like Him. Their eyes would be opened, and they would live forever (Genesis 3:5-6). The result was a race banished from the garden and put under a curse.

The temptation to declare our independence from the one true God and to function as gods ourselves is at the heart of the New Age. In this way, the New Age is nothing new. It repackages an ancient and deadly error.

3. A race banished from the garden can never be restored by turning inward. When we turn inward, all we find is sin. Our fallen condition demands that we turn to God himself for salvation.

Though the New Age teaches that our problems are rooted in our ignorance of our divine potential, the Scriptures teach that our problems are rooted in our sin against a holy God.

Jesus was clear about what unrepentant humanity finds when it turns inward. "From within, out of men's hearts, come evil thoughts, sexual immorality, theft, murder, adultery, greed, malice, deceit, lewdness, envy, slander, arrogance and folly. All these evils come from inside and make a man 'unclean'" (Mark 7:21-23).

The answer to the problem of sin is not meditation or yoga or some consciousness-raising therapy. The answer is repentance from sin and faith in Jesus Christ as Lord and Savior. We cannot find forgiveness of sin or eternal life by looking within.

Neither can we hope to find enlightenment through reincarnation. The writer of Hebrews tells us that we have but one earthly life, after which comes judgment (Hebrews 9:27). The Bible teaches the resurrection of the redeemed and the damned at the end of history; it does not teach reincarnation.

4. Contrary to the New Age teaching, Jesus is not an example of someone who tapped into divine power in the same way that anyone can. Jesus made claims that singled Him out from all other spiritual teachers. He said, "I am the way and the truth and the life. No one comes to the Father except through me" (John 14:6).

He backed up those claims with a miraculous ministry of healing the sick, casting out demons, and even raising the dead. He predicted His own crucifixion and resurrection from the dead. Through His resurrection, Paul tells us, Jesus was "declared to be the Son of God with power" (Romans 1:4, KJV).

Jesus stands unique in the history of the world. No wonder Peter said, "Salvation is found in no one else, for there is no other name under heaven given to men by which we must be saved" (Acts 4:12).

5. The Bible clearly condemns as "detestable" the occult practices so in vogue with New Agers (Deuteronomy 18:10-12). Paul lists witchcraft and idolatry as works of "the sinful nature" and not of the Spirit (Galatians 5:19-20).

Supernatural experiences may come from God. But they may also come from Satan and demons. Paul warns us that Satan himself masquerades as an angel of light (2 Corinthians 11:14). What may seem good or spiritual may be fueled by the evil one himself.

WITNESSING TO NEW AGERS

Christians should first understand that reaching out to those in the New Age involves spiritual warfare. This is serious business. But we can find comfort in realizing our position of spiritual victory in Christ.

Before engaging in spiritual battle and trying to win those who have been taken captive to the New Age, Christians have to arm themselves with Scripture. We need to know what we believe about God, Christ, sin, and salvation. And we need to be able to find Bible passages to support these beliefs.

God will speak to New Agers through His Word (Hebrews 4:12-13).

I have one more suggestion. Since New Agers don't believe in a personal God, Christians should stress that God is personal. We know He is because of His love. He sent His Son to die for our sins. No impersonal Life Force is capable of such radical love.

So, as we reach out to New Agers, this should be our message: "God so loved the world . . ." (John 3:16).

Transcendental Meditation

HOW IT GOT STARTED

In 1959 Maharishi Mahesh Yogi flew to California from India as a Hindu missionary to the West. A few months later he founded the Spiritual Regeneration Movement in Los Angeles. By the early '70s, people were flocking to him to learn his technique for getting the most out of their mental potential.

KEY ATTRACTIONS

Transcendental meditation (TM) conceals that its roots are sunk deep in Hinduism. Instead, for our secular society, it describes itself as a scientific technique of relaxation that promotes health, increases intelligence, and improves personal relationships by reducing inner stress.

WHERE IT PARTS COMPANY WITH CHRISTIANITY

TM teaches that all creation is divine, and that the Supreme Being is not personal. Initiation into TM includes a ritual of idol worship, in which the person brings offerings for Maharishi's dead teacher. TM's technique of relaxation calls for mentally reciting a mantra —a word or syllable associated with a Hindu god.

STATUS TODAY

TM says that since Maharishi arrived in California 30 years ago, the movement has trained about 2 million meditators in the U.S. and over 3 million worldwide. Recruitment is down to about 5,000 a year, but TM continues to advertise.[1]

David Haddon is a technical editor in the San Francisco Bay area. He is also a free-lance writer who has specialized in analyzing Eastern religious groups and mysticism. He wrote a book on TM and contributed a chapter on it for A Guide to Cults and New Religions *(InterVarsity Press).*

Transcendental Meditation:
It's More than Relaxation

By DAVID HADDON

SOON AFTER I WENT TO WORK as an editor of industrial and technical publications in the San Francisco Bay area, an Iranian engineer at my office asked me, "Are you a meditator? You always seem so peaceful."

I told her the peace she had seen in me came from my relationship with Jesus Christ. She had been searching for peace through transcendental meditation (TM). And she was guessing I had received my peace from TM.

This engineer is just one of many people I have known who practice either TM or one of the similar Hindu or New Age religions.

Most of these groups share TM's belief in what is called pantheism, or monism ("All is One"). They teach that humans, and the rest of creation, are divine, and that "God" is not personal. Each part of creation, they say, is like a single cell that, together, make up "God," the impersonal Absolute.

Most people don't think of C. S. Lewis as a prophet. But in his book *Miracles,* he said the real battle for the hearts and minds of people would not be between communism and capitalism. It would be between pantheism and the Christian faith. The current popularity of Hindu-based religions, such as TM, the New Age, and Unity, shows how prophetic Lewis' words were.

HOW TM GOT A FOOTHOLD

When Maharishi Mahesh Yogi (mah-ha-RISH-ee MA-heesh YOH-ghee) came to the United States, he didn't hide the Hindu roots of his teachings. He talked about the Hindu goal of breaking the chain of reincarnation and reaching bliss-consciousness in this life. And he gave his disciples one-word or one-syllable mantras to mentally recite each day. Some of these mantras were even the names of Hindu gods.

By the late '60s, he realized that practical-minded Americans weren't responding well to this religious approach. So he switched from promoting TM as the fast track to bliss-consciousness to promoting it as a way to a better life right now.

Then, in the early '70s, some scientific studies reported that TM decreased heart and breathing rates and increased alpha brain waves. These reports appeared in journals like the *Scientific American.*

The premature evaluation was that TM was a good way to relax. So public schools and universities began teaching TM as a relaxation technique. TM became a fad. And Maharishi presented himself as the messiah who would bring world peace through TM.

In 1976 a group of New Jersey Christians filed suit to stop the public schools from teaching TM. They argued it was a religion. So it was unconstitutional for the federal government to pay the $41,000 for the teaching materials and for the state government to use them to teach TM.

In December of 1977, the judge said he agreed and that TM was a form of Hindu religion.

This federal court ruling dampened Maharishi's hope of using the government to promote TM. But he switched strategies again. This time he claimed he could teach TMers occult powers like levitation, disappearing, and passing through walls. This backfired on Maharishi. It cost TM much of its credibility among the scientific community.

Today, TM continues to promote itself as nonreligious. In a half-page ad in the *Kansas City Star* it invites people to a free introductory lecture and says, "TM doesn't require any change in your religion." It adds, "Transcendental meditation is nothing more than a technique to help you get the most out of your mental potential. So you can develop incredibly clear, creative thinking."

"There's also reduced stress," the ad says. "Lower blood pressure. Longer lifespan. And all-around better health."[2] The ad says the beneficial effects of TM have been proven by studies at Harvard, Stanford, and other renowned institutions. These studies have since been challenged by groups ranging from the Stanford Research Institute to the German federal government.

While TM continues to seek recruits, TM leaders also take active TMers into advanced—and expensive—courses involving occult practices such as Hindu astrology. Indian medicine, herbal supplements, and crystals "with healing powers" have also been added to the TM line, for the health conscious.

FRAUD AND NEGLIGENCE SUITS

In the last few years, some long-term TMers suffering from what they and their doctors believe are TM-related disorders have sued TM and Maharishi for fraud and negligence.

They have charged fraud over false claims made by TM. And they have charged negligence over being advised to do more meditation whenever they complained of mental and emotional problems arising from their meditation.

Robert Kropinski, for example, received a judgment for $138,000. One psychologist testified that Kropinski, after meditating 40 hours a week for 11 years, scored 20 points lower on an IQ test than he had when in high school. (Kropinski's case was later reversed and is scheduled for retrial.)

Joe Kelly, whose suit was settled out of court, told me about his problems at work in a sprout-raising business owned and run by fellow TMers. He and another TMer responsible for programming the automatic watering system both kept forgetting to program the system. Time and again the sprouts were either drowned or dried out. Joe says, "I would have fired me if I had been manager . . . but the guy who ran the company forgot to program the system too. So it became more like a situation comedy than a business."

By the late '80s, American psychologists had studied enough mental cases to conclude that programs like TM, which use mind-emptying meditation and deep breathing, tend to produce people who suffer from panic attacks, forgetfulness, and inability to concentrate.[3]

The response of TM to these charges has been to require initiates to sign release forms to protect from lawsuits.

TM still refuses to tell would-be TMers that the initiation ceremony is a Hindu ritual. Nor do they explain that this ritual involves worshiping a picture of Maharishi's dead master from India, Guru Dev.

THE INITIATION RITUAL

To begin TM, a person attends two free, introductory lectures that present TM as a nonreligious mental technique. Next, candidates for initiation pay their fee of about $400 and are told to bring flowers, fruit, and a white handkerchief. At the ceremony, in a candlelit room filled with incense, these "offerings" are laid on an altar before the picture of Guru Dev.

During this worship ritual of initiation, the teacher implants in the candidate's mind a sound that invokes a Hindu deity. The new TMer is not aware of it, but this is the secret purpose of the sound the TMer will mentally recite each day.

Ex-TM teacher Greg Randolph, whom I met some years ago, says that among the 16 mantras he assigned to people were sounds like: eng, em, enga, hirim, hiring, shirim, and sham. These are not the actual names of deities but are supposed to invoke various Hindu gods.

To help implant the mantra, the teacher uses the Sanskrit language to sing a hymn to Guru Dev. This song worships the dead guru as a manifestation of many gods including the main Hindu gods Brahma, Vishnu, and Shiva. Here's an excerpt of the song, translated into English:

Guru in the glory of Brahma, Guru in the glory of Vishnu . . . to Shri Guru Dev adorned with glory, I bow down.

Ex-TMer Joe Kelly described for me the impact the hymn of worship had on him:

By the end of the song, I was somewhere else where I had never been before. I thought this was the same type of experience [as drugs], but controllable. So I thought, Well, this is great, this is wonderful.

Not every TMer has a similar experience, but Joe's reaction shows the power of the ceremony to alter the mind.

After the hymn, the teacher whispers to the initiate the secret mantra. (Maharishi has given the impression that the mantras are specially chosen for each person. In fact, they are assigned according to the person's age and sex.) The teacher tells the TMer to mentally recite it for 20 minutes twice a day—for starters.

As much as possible, TM disguises the religious side of this ceremony. For a parallel example, imagine a Christian having someone over to her apartment for a Bible study, inviting her guest into the pool for a swim, and then—in Greek—baptizing the guest in the name of the Father, Son, and Holy Spirit. Farfetched? Not when you realize that the initiation ceremony is to TM what baptism is to Christian faith: the ritual of entry.

THE DANGERS OF MEDITATION

This ritual, enacted kneeling before a picture of Guru Dev, and complete with offerings of flowers, fruit, and a handkerchief, points up the relevance of New Testament warnings against idolatry. Paul explained that "the sacrifices of pagans are offered to demons" (1 Corinthians 10:20).

Former TM teacher Vail Hamilton, working with me on the book *TM Wants You* (Baker), tells of spirits she encountered. She said, "I began to become aware of the presence of spirit beings on either side of me when I was meditating. . . . Once I looked at one of them, and I saw a small dark creature with sharp teeth."

Christians and Hindus both believe that such spirits exist.

We open our minds to demons when we practice the meditative technique of TM, which clears the mind of conscious thought. This empty-minded state is similar to that used by channelers to gain contact with their familiar spirits.

Anyone doing this kind of meditation runs the risk of receiving evil spirits and becoming demonized. This is one of the reasons mind-emptying meditation is not acceptable to Christians. Even the name of Jesus can be misused as a mantra. When we use His name this way, we disregard His command to avoid "meaningless repetition" in prayer (Matthew 6:7, NASB).

As Christians, we do need to quietly meditate on Scripture and on God. But clearing our minds of all thought leads to a dangerous mental passivity.

SHARING CHRIST WITH TM FOLLOWERS

TM and other Hindu-based cults appeal to a fallen humanity that wants to believe we are gods and are not responsible to anyone but ourselves.

I recently visited the TM center at Berkeley and shared my personal testimony with a TM teacher. I told him about my life-changing experience with Christ. The teacher respectfully told me that I had experienced "God" at the level of the man who says, "I am Lord of all I survey."

I replied, "I'm not Lord. Jesus is Lord."

The man had completely misunderstood what I said in my testimony. Communication with TMers is difficult because they use some of the same words we do, but with different meaning. I shared with him the Christian doctrines of the resurrection of the body and of the last judgment. This clarified that the Bible teaches the eternity of personal existence. For him, by contrast, the goal of life is to reach a level of enlightenment that allows him to break free of the cycle of reincarnation. When that happens, he believes, death will free him from personality and consciousness. His personhood will be forever lost in the impersonal Absolute, or cosmos.

So one thing TMers need to hear about is the hope of eternal personal existence.

As you witness to TMers, try to prick their conscience by pointing out the deceptive way people are led into the ritual initiation. And pray for the Holy Spirit to do His job of convicting about sin, righteousness, and judgment.

There is hope even for TMers who live under the delusion of their own divinity and who believe that "God" is not a Person. For when Jesus said, "I am the way and the truth," He presented himself as the only way to the person of God the Father.

In contrast, TM offers only an end of personality in an impersonal Absolute. But as human beings made in the image of the personal God, no one can ever be fully satisfied by anything less than a personal relationship with our personal Creator.

As Christians we should confidently share the privilege of knowing Jesus Christ personally. "God was pleased to have all his fullness dwell in him [Jesus], and through him to reconcile to himself all things . . . by making peace through his blood, shed on the cross" (Colossians 1:19-20). This is the message of reconciliation that every Hindu needs to hear.

---

1. Leslie Goldberg, "Finding 'Heaven on the Outside,'" part 2 of a 2-part series, *San Francisco Examiner,* September 11, 1989.

2. April 20, 1990, A-5.

3. Margaret Thaler Singer and Richard Ofshe, "Thought Reform Programs and the Production of Psychiatric Casualties," *Psychiatric Annals* (April 1990): 188-93.

10

Unification Church

AT A GLANCE

HOW IT GOT STARTED

Sun Myung Moon founded the church in 1954, in Korea. He says that on Easter of 1936, when he was 16, Jesus Christ called him to complete the mission He himself had failed.

KEY ATTRACTIONS

This is a dynamic, loving group that offers people the opportunity to change the world through following a powerful, influential religious visionary.

WHERE IT PARTS COMPANY WITH CHRISTIANITY

Moon says he is the fulfillment of the Second Coming. He says he holds a position greater than Jesus, that Jesus was not physically raised from the dead, and that Moon's own book, *Divine Principle*, is a new revelation with more authority than the Bible.

STATUS TODAY

The church is strongest in Korea and Japan, with several hundred thousand members. In America, there are less than 10,000 active members, with the world headquarters in New York City.

James Beverley is a professor of theology and ethics at Ontario Theological Seminary, Toronto. He has studied the Unification church for over a decade and has recently written a chapter on the subject for Evangelizing the Cults (Servant Publications).

The Unification Church:

A New Messiah

BY JAMES A. BEVERLEY

YOU WOULD NOTICE something strange about these wedding pictures. Anyone would. The bride is there; she looks beautiful and happy. That's true. There are lots of smiling guests. True again. And the groom is in the picture. Yes, literally.

When Hoon Sook Pak married Heung Jin on February 20, 1984, she had to be content with just his picture. He died in a traffic crash seven weeks earlier.

So why the wedding? Rev. Sun Myung Moon wanted his deceased son married. And a willing disciple obliged.

A couple years ago I met a Unificationist* who attended this wedding. She told me it was the most beautiful ceremony she had ever seen. She said she trusted Rev. Moon's leadership, and she was inspired by the dedication of Hoon Sook.

I admire Hoon Sook's commitment too. Most of the Unificationists I've met are dedicated. They often put evangelical

*Members of the Unification church have also been known as Moonies, a term they consider offensive.

Christians to shame by their hard work. Their zeal has challenged me.

I wish I could tell you the Unificationists are a great group of Bible-believing Christians. I wish I could tell you they trust in Jesus Christ as their only Lord and Savior. And I would like to tell you they believe the historic Christian faith.

But I can't. It would be untrue.

Please don't misunderstand my criticism. First of all, I support freedom of religion. I defend every Unificationist's right to believe in Moon as the messiah. Second, I try hard in my research to be fair and accurate. So, I don't automatically accept every nasty rumor I hear about Moon. For example, I know that Moon does not own Proctor and Gamble, as some rumors claim. Nor does he have special hypnotic powers that help him brainwash his followers.

So why do people follow him? After all, he did serve 13 months in prison in 1984-85 for tax evasion.

I can think of several bright, gifted Unificationists I have met at academic conferences who would love to answer the question.

I expect they would remind us that many evangelicals, like Jerry Falwell, say the U.S. government unjustly persecuted Moon on the income tax case. They might also remind us of Moon's generosity; the Unification church has helped pay college costs for many of its members.

Moon's followers might explain to us that Jesus came to the Korean prophet in 1936 and asked him to complete the Christian mission in Korea. And they might say they believe in Jesus, trust the Bible, and want to unite with all Christians. They might even close out their answer by encouraging us to be open to Rev. Moon, and not to be close-minded to the messiah and his new revelations, like the Pharisees were with Jesus.

One of the biggest attractions to the Unification church is that Moon has a wide-ranging program to improve the world. He owns the *Washington Times,* one of the more influential newspapers in America. He is a business leader in South Korea and has recently been appointed head of all the clans in his native country. He has started ballet companies and symphonies. He has tried to improve the moral climate of North America by taking a stand against drugs and other social evils. He has funded conferences for religious leaders, politicians, scientists, and the news media. And his followers often speak of his powerful understanding of Scripture and his radical commitment to unselfish service to humanity.

Sounds pretty impressive, doesn't it?

I don't mind admitting it. Cult leaders often accomplish a lot, and some of them do it with real class. Christians can learn a lot from the hard work and dedication of the Unificationists and their leader. Rev. Moon has a broad and diverse vision, and he knows how to make a difference.

However, starting ballet companies and owning newspapers and having conferences for religious leaders doesn't make Moon or his followers Christian.

Neither are they Christian just because they say they follow Jesus and believe the Bible. Cult leaders are not likely to tell you they are against Jesus and they don't really obey the Bible. Jesus warned about the subtleness of false prophets (Matthew 7:15).

10 CRITICISMS

It's time for some blunt talk. I want to be fair to the Unificationists. That's why I've cleared up some false rumors about them and talked about some of the good things Moon has done.

But I have 10 major objections to Moon's teaching.

1. He is wrong about God. Moon denies the Trinity, the personality of the Holy Spirit, and the full deity of Jesus.

2. He is wrong about the birth of Jesus. Moon denies the Virgin Birth and teaches that Zechariah was the father of Jesus. This adulterous affair by John the Baptist's father caused severe tension between Joseph and Mary, Moon says.

In fact, Moon says, Joseph resented Jesus so much he deliberately left the 12-year-old Boy at the Jerusalem Temple when it came time to return to Nazareth (see Luke 2:41-48 for a different version).

3. He is wrong about the death of Christ. Moon says Jesus was supposed to find a bride, get married, and start the perfect family. The failure of Jesus to do this, and the failure of the Jews to believe He was the Messiah, led to Calvary.

4. He is wrong about the resurrection of Christ. Moon denies the bodily resurrection of Jesus and says His body was delivered to Satan.

5. He is wrong about the second coming of Christ. He denies that Jesus will return. He says the New Testament teaches a messiah will come. But Moon says Jesus was the Messiah for the New Testament age, and that Moon is the messiah for the Completed Testament age. The theory that Moon fulfills the second coming of Christ is directly opposed to what the Bible says (see Acts 1:11).

6. He is wrong about the Bible. He denies the Bible's unique authority. He says his work, *Divine Principle,* is more important than the Bible.

7. He is wrong about the Final Judgment. He denies the Bible's teaching about hell, and he teaches that everyone will be saved eventually, including Satan.

8. He is wrong about salvation. He denies the full sufficiency of Christ's death, teaches that salvation is by works, and says that salvation comes through following him and his wife as True Parents. Moon says he is sinless.

9. He is wrong about prophecy. Moon tries to predict the future, but he has made false prophecies about himself, his followers, and world events. For example, he predicted that communism would be overcome in 1980. He also predicted a new world order would begin in 1981. When that didn't happen, he extended the date another 21 years.

10. He is wrong about holiness. Moon says that to be holy, we must use his Holy Salt on food, drink his Holy Wine

as part of the initiation into his church, pray on his Holy Grounds (various world sites he has blessed), and follow his Holy Days. His followers must carry his picture for protection, learn his Korean language (which he says will be the language of heaven), and bow to him.

10 COMMANDMENTS

If these 10 criticisms are as accurate as I believe they are, how can we convince Unificationists to accept the true gospel?

Let me suggest what I call "Ten Commandments for Truth Tellers."

1. Focus on Jesus Christ. I mention Jesus at the outset because it is so easy to get lost in debate and to forget to point people to the Lord. I remember the evening a member of a cult group came to my door a few years ago; we ended up in a shouting match. This expert on cults never once told the man about Jesus. Don't make my mistake.

2. Be loving and kind.

3. Base your witness on a genuine Christian life, backed up by prayer and worship.

4. Be informed about your faith as well as the faith of the person to whom you are witnessing.

5. Use different strategies with different people. Don't lock yourself into one of the many popular evangelism programs.

6. Go to others for help in preparing your witness and in the actual witnessing. That will give you the confidence of knowing you are not in the battle alone. Others are praying for you.

7. Deal with crucial, central issues. Forget about trivialities.

8. Listen to the Unificationists' point of view, and admit any wrong presumptions you may have made. Your criticism needs this kind of openness to correction.

9. Be firm in your stand against beliefs and life-styles that are clearly opposed in the Bible.

10. Be patient, as the Holy Spirit uses your witness.

I believe the Unificationist who comes your way needs you as a special long-term friend. It is going to take time to reorient his spiritual beliefs. You will face long talks about how scary life seems outside the Unification camp. Unificationists are warned about the evil that comes to the deserter.

You and your church will have to replace the intimacy that the Unificationist left behind. Only then will you be able to move on in your ministry to the person. And only then will you be able to show the Unificationist that the Christian Church is committed to winning the world for Jesus Christ, the only Messiah of God.

Isn't it interesting we are back to commitment? I should tell you that Hoon Sook is still married to Heung Jin, and she has gained fame as a ballerina. All of this in honor of Rev. Moon. A friend of mine once said: "Some people are more committed to error than some Christians are to the truth."

I remember the first time I met members of the Unification church. I spent a weekend with them at their seminary in Barrytown, N.Y. I was not impressed by their beliefs or their distortion of clear biblical teaching. But I was impressed by their real commitment. Before I flew home to Canada, I stayed overnight in their world mission center in Manhattan. Reflecting on the zeal of Unificationists led me to rededicate my life to Jesus Christ.

Christians can learn from the Unificationists about real dedication. I pray that the Unificationists will learn from Christians about the real gospel.

I would like to dedicate this chapter to the memory of my uncle, Ivan Lutes (1924-91). A leading deacon at Parkside Baptist Church in Moncton, N.B., he was a faithful witness to the love and grace of the Lord Jesus Christ.

Scientology

AT A GLANCE

HOW IT GOT STARTED

L. Ron Hubbard founded Scientology in 1954. The headquarters is in Los Angeles, and it has offices in most free countries. Hubbard died in 1986, but his cult lives on.

KEY ATTRACTION

Most people join Scientology because it offers quick solutions to lifelong problems. It promises to use space-age technology to identify and eliminate problems such as bad habits and psychosomatic illnesses.

WHERE IT PARTS COMPANY WITH CHRISTIANITY

Hubbard taught there are many gods, that humans can become godlike creatures, and that it is despicable to tell people they need to repent of sin. He said the crucifixion of Jesus is a legend, and the idea of heaven is corny.

STATUS TODAY

Scientologists number somewhere between 2-6 million, worldwide, depending on which Scientologist you quote. Sales of 12 million copies of their heavily advertised book, *Dianetics*, suggest Scientology is growing in numbers and influence.

Kurt Van Gorden directs Utah Gospel Mission, a missionary ministry to cult members. He has trained hundreds of Christians for short-term mission work among the cults of America. He lives with his family in Provo, Utah.

Scientology:

Trillion-Year-Old Thetans

By KURT VAN GORDEN

I HAVE GREAT COMPASSION for members of the Church of Scientology. They are where I once was: in a cult.

I was a member of the Children of God. I had been led to believe a false prophet and his teachings. But a Christian pastor eventually helped me see how unbiblical this supposedly Bible-based cult was.

Yet even after I realized that the teachings of the cult were wrong, I still struggled over whether or not to leave. I fought a battle between knowledge and emotion. My brain told me the religion was false. But my heart reminded me about how much I loved these people. I didn't want to leave them.

My pastor friend assured me that my feelings of love were God-given, and that I could use this love to bring my friends to Christ. It was then that God called me to become a missionary to the cults.

I moved from Ohio to California, to attend Bible school and to work with Dr. Walter R. Martin, a noted author and pioneer in countercult evangelism. It was there I first became introduced to Scientology.

Dr. Martin had released a cassette tape about Scientology. The tape drew threats of a lawsuit by Scientologists. So Dr. Martin assigned me to document the accuracy of the tape.

I read about 75 Scientology books and hundreds of pages

from files. The more I studied their beliefs, the more I grew to love these people for Christ's sake. I understand so well the dilemma many of them face. I have found, through my witnessing experiences with Scientologists, many of them have seen the logical contradictions in their belief system that I had had in mine. What holds them bound to the cult is what held me to the Children of God: emotional attachment to the group. They fight the same battle I did between knowledge and emotion.

HEADQUARTERS: HOLLYWOOD

The Church of Scientology owns a tall hotel and office building on Hollywood Boulevard in Hollywood, Calif.

As a new Christian, I used to stand on this famous street and give out gospel tracts. Sometimes I would see young Scientologists standing in front of their building. They would be holding clipboards and asking the passersby if they wanted a free personality test. The test would show personality flaws Scientology said it could eliminate.

Usually, when I saw this going on, I would walk over and stand by the Scientologists. I have entered into lengthy conversations with these recruiters and with people to whom they were giving personality tests. Some of the people getting a free personality test were unsuspecting Christians visiting town. These people attended church, but many didn't know enough about their faith to be able to quickly identify the distorted teachings of the Scientologist.

So I would ask the Scientologist questions that would help passersby quickly see Scientology as the unbiblical cult it is.

Scientology calls itself a "world religion emerging in the space age." It prides itself on the new "technologies" and electronic devices it uses for "religious counseling purposes."

Lafayette Ronald Hubbard (1911-86), the founder of Scientology, was a popular science fiction writer of the 1930s and 1940s. His novels reflect his resourcefulness in drawing from his experiences in travel, reading, and scientific research. These experiences, blended with his wild and flowing imagination, held science fiction readers as spellbound as any movie would today.

L. Ron Hubbard's science fiction career came to an end when he shifted his attention to religion. We aren't certain why he made the switch. But we do know *Time* magazine reported that Hubbard said this to a writers' convention in 1949: "If a man really wants to make a million dollars, the best way would be to start his own religion" (April 5, 1976, 57).

Hubbard was successful both in starting a religion and in becoming a millionaire.

His first book on religion began a religious movement that later became the Church of Scientology. The book, published in May 1950, was *Dianetics: The Modern Science of Mental Health*. Through over four decades of promotional work, the book has sold more than 12 million copies. Celebrities who have helped promote it include John Travolta, Karen Black, Joe Namath, and jazz musicians Chick Corea and Stanley Clark. Other well-known Scientologists include Kirstie Alley and Priscilla Presley.

Some followers of Dianetics (which means "through the soul") claim that the Dianetic theory contained in the book produced remarkable results. Hubbard wrote that his new "science of mind" could rid a person of "psychoses, neuroses, compulsions and repressions . . . any autogenic (self-generated) diseases referred to as psychosomatic ills" (1986 ed., 14).

Critics of Dianetics wasted no time in refuting the unscientific conclusions of the practice. The first concerted action against Dianetics was by the American Psychological Association at their September 1950 meeting. A resolution, adopted unanimously by the 8,000 members, said Hubbard's claims for Dianetics "are not supported by empirical evidence of the sort required for the establishment of scientific generalizations."

The Dianetics movement merged into the Church of Scientology, incorporated by Hubbard in 1954. Scientology, which means "study of knowledge," contains a complicated system of beliefs that is hard to condense to paper. This is mainly due to the prolific hand of Hubbard. He wrote over 100 books to further the cause of Scientology. He added to that thousands of pages of staff communications.

TRILLION-YEAR-OLD THETANS

If you were to walk up to a Scientologist and ask what his beliefs are, more than likely you would not get a clear answer. Scientology has its own vocabulary, and you'll not find their words in a common dictionary.

For example, a Scientologist will say, "You are not your body." According to them, you are a thetan (THAY-ten). The thetan is a spirit being similar to the soul, and it has existed for some 300 trillion years. The thetan has spent most of these trillions of years entering bodies on different planets of the universe, only to die and reincarnate on another planet.

The problem for the Scientologist is that each past life had aberrations and bad experiences, called engrams. The engrams attach to the thetan like barnacles to a ship. And the presence of these engrams affect the life journey of a person, causing the person to react in self-destructive ways to society.

The solution for the Scientologist is to get rid of these engrams and become "clear." This release from the barnacles of past lives allows the person smooth sailing above the insanities of society.

But how can the Scientologist detect the engrams attached to his thetan? Hubbard came up with an electronic device called the E-meter. During a counseling procedure called "auditing," the "preclear" (one who is not yet clear of the engrams) holds two tin cans with wires attached to the E-meter. The auditor watches the E-meter, while asking questions of the preclear. The E-meter is supposed to detect internal responses to the questions. And this helps the auditor locate chains of engrams.

This, and other technical courses offered by the church, assist the preclear on their spiritual journey. The goal is to erase the engrams and obtain the benefits of being clear.

One benefit of becoming clear is that the Scientologist can move on to become an "operating thetan." This ends the person's cycle of reincarnation and transforms the Scientologist into a *homo novis*—a godlike being. Hubbard's writings do not clarify how this change happens, or where these godlike creatures go after they leave this life.

But in this life, the operating thetan is supposed to be free of mind-generated illnesses and free from making self-destructive decisions. In addition, the operating thetan is supposed to have control over matter, energy, space, and time.

One other interesting trait is that the operating thetan supposedly remembers all of his previous lives, whether on earth or on other planets. Some Scientologists say they remember their evolution, from jellyfish, to clam, to bird, to Piltdown man, to Homo sapiens.

This seems utterly amazing to those who have studied evolutionary claims. The Piltdown man, for example, was a hoax pulled off by British scientists in the early 1900s. They joined a skullcap of a man with a jawbone of a chimpanzee. The scientific community didn't discover the fraud until 1953, after Hubbard had already included the Piltdown man in his published cycle of evolution. Plainly, the Piltdown man does not exist and never has existed. That, of course, raises questions about the accuracy of what Scientologists say they remember about their past lives.

SCIENTOLOGISTS DENY GOD

What does Scientology say about God and the Christian faith?

God. Their writings certainly deny the God of the Bible. The Bible clearly teaches that only one true God exists (Deuteronomy 6:4). The Bible also tells us that God abhors the teaching that many gods exist (Joshua 24:23).

Hubbard once wrote in *Professional Auditor's Bulletin,* "There are gods above all other gods, and gods beyond the gods of the universes."

The Australian Parliament released a study on Scientology in 1968. The study quoted many of Hubbard's staff communications. These revealed his mockery of heaven and his denial of the biblical God. Hubbard wrote, "For a long while some people have been cross with me for my lack of cooperating in believing in a Christian heaven, God and Christ. I never said I didn't believe in a big Thetan, but there was certainly something very corny about heaven, et al."

Jesus. Hubbard had no few things to say about Jesus Christ. In the book *Scientology: A World Religion Emerges in the Space Age,* Hubbard said, "It is believed by many authorities that Jesus was a member of the cult of the Essenes, who believed in reincarnation." Hubbard didn't identify his sources. But when we examine the Bible, an authoritative source on Jesus, we find that He lived in Nazareth nearly all His life (Luke 4:16). The Essenes were a group of Jews who lived in a monastic community near Jerusalem.

As for the idea that Jesus believed in reincarnation, we find the opposite in His teachings. He taught that He was the only one who preexisted: "You are from below; I am from above. You are of this world; I am not of this world" (John 8:23). Humans did not come from above, as taught in reincarnation. The composition of humanity began in the Garden of Eden, when we were created by God.

Hubbard's disrespect for Jesus is obvious, since Hubbard places Jesus at a lower spiritual level than him and other Scientologists. In *Certainty Magazine* he wrote, "Neither Lord Buddha nor Jesus Christ were OT [operating thetans] according to the evidence. They were just a shade above clear."

Hubbard went on to deny Christ and the Cross in his *Professional Auditor's Bulletin.* Hubbard called the story of the

Crucifixion a legend and an implant, or warped understanding, in preclears.

"You will find the cross as a symbol all over the universe, and the Christ legend as an implant in preclears a million years ago."

Sin. Hubbard went on to reject the biblical concept of humanity's evil: "It is despicable and utterly beneath contempt to tell a man he must repent, that he is evil."

The Bible condemns Hubbard's teachings. "Who is the liar? It is the man who denies that Jesus is the Christ. Such a man is the antichrist—he denies the Father and the Son" (1 John 2:22). When we look to the Bible, we find that Jesus not only called men evil but also told men to repent (see Matthew 7:11; 4:17).

Salvation. The Bible and Scientology also disagree about salvation. According to Scientology, salvation means being released from the cycle of birth and death. It means leaving behind this cycle of reincarnation and taking on the godlike characteristics of an operating thetan.

But according to the Bible, salvation is an experience we enjoy when we place our faith in the person and work of Jesus Christ (Romans 10:9-10; Acts 4:10-12). The sacrifice of Jesus cleanses us from our sins if we believe on Him for our salvation.

The biblical teaching about salvation also clashes with Scientology's teaching about reincarnation. The Book of Hebrews says, "Man is destined to die once, and after that to face judgment" (9:27). There is no second, third, or fourth chance after this life. Only judgment awaits us, followed by reward or punishment.

A MESSAGE FOR SCIENTOLOGISTS

Every Scientologist needs to hear the message of the saving grace of the Lord Jesus Christ. They can leave behind their works of trying to overcome the effects of hypothetical past lives.

Scripture triumphantly tells us, "For it is by grace you have been saved, through faith—and this not from yourselves, it is the gift of God—not by works, so that no one can boast" (Ephesians 2:8-9).

I have led several Scientologists to the Lord by helping them study the Bible. Scientologists do not understand about forgiveness of sins. Otherwise, they would not be trying to erase their engrams.

We can help Scientologists by showing them the contrast between forgiveness and unforgiveness, reincarnation and resurrection, Jesus and false prophets. The gift of salvation through Jesus is a message every Scientologist needs to hear.

Satanism

AT A GLANCE

HOW IT GOT STARTED

The worship of Satan is as ancient as humanity. But the father of satanic practices in this century is Anton LaVey. In 1966 he organized the Church of Satan in San Francisco. Three years later he published *The Satanic Bible.*

KEY ATTRACTIONS

Satanism attracts the angry and the powerless—those who don't feel they fit in anywhere. They are lured by promises of power, sex, friendship, and drugs.

WHERE IT PARTS COMPANY WITH CHRISTIANITY

Satanism takes nearly every basic Christian teaching and reverses it. For example, it lauds greed and revenge. It says humans are just another species of animal.

STATUS TODAY

It is impossible to tell how many satanists there are. Estimates run as high as 10,000 covens, or small groups of Satan worshipers, in just North America. From the number of occult-related crimes, and testimonies of ex-satanists, it appears the movement is growing.

Jerry Johnston is an evangelist and author who has done extensive research into satanism and other issues facing young people. He wrote The Edge of Evil: The Rise of Satanism in North America *(Word Publishing). He lives in Overland Park, Kans.*

Satanism:
Christianity Reversed

By JERRY JOHNSTON

A FEW MONTHS AGO I stood over the comatose body of an 18-year-old man. His name was Michael.

Tattooed on his body were satanic markings, such as pentagrams—five-pointed stars used in satanic rituals.

Months earlier, Michael had written a letter to Ozzy Osborne, the prince of heavy-metal music. Michael said he wanted to reign in hell with the devil. After he wrote the letter, he hung himself. He dangled from the rope long enough to cause brain damage. Now, attached to a ventilator, he lies in a nursing home.

I don't know how Michael got involved in the occult. But I do know that some experts in adolescence estimate that 10 percent of American young people are dabbling in satanism. And of those who dabble, 1 to 3 percent become more heavily involved.

The worship of Satan, or the occult, is as ancient as humanity. But satanism got a boost on April 30, 1966. That's when former police photographer Anton LaVey announced the birth of the Church of Satan. Most people took little notice of LaVey and his plans to grow a church. They figured he was just another San Francisco fanatic.

Three years later LaVey put definition to his dream by penning the now famous *Satanic Bible*. This manual of how to worship Satan has sold nearly a million copies and is approaching its 30th printing.

113

LaVey's ideas are not all original. Much of his inspiration and material came from Edward Alexander Crowley, born in 1875 in the United Kingdom. This son of devout Plymouth Brethren parents so shocked people with his teachings that he earned the dubious nickname The Beast. It was a title he said he proudly claimed.

Crowley was an avid worshiper of Satan. From his extensive writing are these two quotes that sum up his teaching: "Do what thou wilt shall be the whole of the law." "Good is evil and evil is good."

Crowley believed, preached, and some say even practiced human sacrifice. In fact, he has been accused of sacrificing his grown son, who was killed in a bizarre ritual that seems to have been part of a Black Mass. Much of today's North American satanism is rooted in the words of both Anton LaVey and Alexander Crowley. From both men sprang voluminous writing, much of which is boring and abstract.

Yet, these writings have carried satanism to higher levels of popularity. The nation's headlines bear witness to this. We read in our newspapers about occult symbols left at crime scenes, human sacrifice (several people on death row admit to killing in Satan's name), sexual and physical abuse related to the occult, child abduction, and the butchery of animals.

Many police officers in the United States and Canada are trained to recognize clues to satanic activity. Several police bureaus now employ undercover agents who specialize in cracking satanic crime. Mental health professionals in most large communities, though mute publicly, are counseling victims of satanic abuse.

Hartgrove Hospital in Chicago opened the country's first Ritualistic Deviant Recovery Center, for people who were trying to defect from satanic activity. This mental health response has been duplicated in centers across North America.

I've talked with police, health care workers, social service employees, lawyers, and ministers who all attest to the reality of this growing religion.

Amazingly the FBI's Behavioral Science Unit still denies evidence of satanic cults in the U.S. Dr. Ted Gunderson, a 30-year FBI veteran, who for 15 years presided over the Los Angeles Bureau with its 700 agents and $22 million annual budget, told me he is mystified by this denial. But he reminded me that until 1956, the official position of the FBI was that there was no Mafia.

WHAT SATANISTS BELIEVE

These nine statements, from *The Satanic Bible*, outline the heart of LaVey's gospel:

1. Satan represents indulgence, instead of abstinence.
2. Satan represents vital existence, instead of spiritual pipe dreams.
3. Satan represents undefiled wisdom, instead of hypocritical self-deceit.
4. Satan represents kindness to those who deserve it, instead of love wasted on ingrates.
5. Satan represents vengeance, instead of turning the other cheek.
6. Satan represents responsibility to the responsible, instead of concern for psychic vampires.
7. Satan represents man as just another animal, sometimes better, more often worse than those that walk on all fours, who, because of his divine spiritual and intellectual development, has become the most vicious animal of all.
8. Satan represents all of the so-called sins, as they lead to physical, mental, or emotional gratification.
9. Satan has been the best friend the church has ever had, as he has kept it in business all these years.

It is easy to see the sensually gratifying philosophy that would appeal especially to rebellious young people. LaVey has said, "This is a very selfish religion. We believe in greed, we believe in selfishness, we believe in all the lustful thoughts that motivate man, because this is man's natural feeling."

Satanism is Christianity in reverse—and not only theo-logically. Satanists memorize the Lord's Prayer backward, they quote Psalm 23 backward. They sometimes even spell back-ward. They'll spell "NATAS," backward for Satan, and "LIVE," backward for evil.

They also distort the Old Testament sacrificial system and mutilate and kill animals and humans for wicked reasons.

According to LaVey's writings, there are three primary rit-uals satanists practice. These rituals are as important to satan-ists as baptism and the Lord's Supper are to Christians.

The rituals are: the compassion ritual (to help someone), the hex ritual (to hurt someone), and the love ritual (to put a spell on someone you want).

The compassion ritual views Lucifer as a benevolent be-ing, ready to help those truly devoted to him. This ritual is practiced by satanists to help someone else facing problems such as those related to health, finances, or education.

The hex ritual reveals the vindictiveness of satanists. Ac-cording to satanists, the target of the hex does not have to be-lieve in magical forces. According to LaVey, most hex rituals are performed in the early morning hours, or about two hours before the target awakes. This is when the subconscious mind is dreaming and is more susceptible to outside influences.

The love ritual is simply erotica in action, unleashed in coven meetings through ritual performances. The person per-forming the rite engages in sex as part of the ritual. Ten sa-tanic holidays that feature this kind of sexual behavior are:

January 17	Satanic Revels
February 2	Satanic Revels
March 20	Equinox Feast Day
June 21	Solstice Feast Day
August 3	Satanic Revels
September 7	Marriage to the Beast
September 22	Equinox Feast Day
November 1	Halloween

November 4   Satanic Revels
December 22   Solstice Feast Day

What happens on these holidays? Ex-satanists report orgies, sex between leaders and inductees, and the impregnation of women "breeders" who produce babies for sacrifice.

Sacrifice plays an important part in satanism. That's because a satanist believes that by killing something, the life force is transferred from the sacrifice to the worshiper. Satanists terrify and torture the sacrifice first, because they believe this increases the life force, much like an adrenaline surge increases a person's strength. Satanists claim they absorb the power of the sacrifice by eating the animal or drinking its blood.

Throughout the year, satanists observe blood ritual holidays. Blood holidays include:

January 7   St. Winebald Day
February 25   St. Walpurgis Day
March 1   St. Eichatadt Day
April 26—May 1   Grand Climax
July 1   Demon Revels
September 20   Midnight Host
October 31   All Hallows' Eve
December 24   High Grand Climax

In public, satanists distance themselves from illegal activity. I am convinced the more dangerous a satanic coven becomes, the more covert, or secretive, their activity.

HUMAN SACRIFICE

Police, ex-satanists, ministers, and hosts of others have speculated on how many people satanists sacrifice each year in America.

Larry Dunn, a Washington State deputy sheriff, and Jacquie Balodis, who counsels ex-satanists, say it is possible devil worshipers sacrifice 50,000 people a year, mostly transients, runaways, and babies from breeders. But that is more than double the 21,500 murders reported by police agencies to the FBI in 1989.

No one could prove that fantastic claim. However, we know that some human sacrifice does occur.

The first substantiated case of satanic murder was a San Francisco case involving Clifford St. Joseph. In 1988 he was convicted of the 1985 occult mutilation murder of a drifter. St. Joseph apparently killed the man during a homosexual satanic rite. The killer sexually molested the victim, carved a pentagram on the man's chest, drained the body of most of its blood, then dripped hot wax into the man's right eye.

Ex-satanists say the reason we don't have more evidence of human sacrifice is because the bodies are usually destroyed, often by burning.

Not only do we know satanists sacrifice humans, we know satanism's teaching permits human sacrifice.

Crowley wrote in his book *Magick,* "For the highest spiritual working one must accordingly choose that victim which contains the greatest and purest force. A male child perfect in innocence and of high intelligence is the most satisfactory and suitable victim. It is a mistake to support that the victim is injured. On the contrary, this is the most blessed and merciful of all deaths, for the elemental spirit is directly built up in the Godhead."

Anton LaVey says, in *The Satanic Bible,* "The only time a satanist would perform a human sacrifice would be if it were to serve a twofold purpose, that being to release the magician's wrath in the throwing of a curse and, more important, to dispose of a totally obnoxious and deserving individual."

Satanic teaching permits human sacrifice. Yet satanists disassociate themselves from criminals who are caught killing people in the name of Satan. I once debated Zeena LaVey, Anton's daughter and now the official spokesperson for the Church of Satan. She said true satanists do not believe in breaking the law.

But how do you believe someone whose theology is the

direct opposite of the Scriptures that say, "Do not lie" (Leviticus 19:11)? As I investigated satanism, the book that kept showing up in occult crimes was *The Satanic Bible,* written by Zeena LaVey's father.

I've also listened to ex-satanists themselves. Sean Sellers, now on death row in McAlister, Okla., told me he killed his mom and dad as a teen satanist. David Wiseman, 17, of Bessemer City, N.C., poured gasoline on himself and set himself aflame in satanic devotion. In his one-page handwritten suicide note found in his bedroom, he said he was going to "live with the devil." Richard Rameriz, the infamous LA Nightstalker, killed 12 in satanic devotion. In a southern California courtroom he hollered out, "Hail Satan." Now convicted, he lives on death row.

HOW TO SPOT A SATANIST

Satanists recruit people many ways. Teenagers are perhaps the most vulnerable—especially those who feel they do not fit in at home or at school. To a disillusioned teen, a "coven" is a pseudofamily. The coven, usually a group of a dozen or less, is secretive, tight-knit, loyal, and protective.

One satanist told me that a recruiter will look for whatever is lacking in a person's life. Then the recruiter will promise to fill this need, be it sex, drugs, power, or companionship.

Veteran police officer Jerry Simandl with the Chicago Police Department says the recruits are drugged, videotaped in sexual acts, and then led in prayer to invite demons into their bodies. The prayer is sealed with a blood ritual, such as the drinking of blood.

If the recruit decides to renege or inform, the videotape becomes a tool of blackmail.

Because satanists are usually secretive, it's not easy to identify them. But there are some warning signs to watch for. Here are a few:

- an expressed interest in the occult
- well-worn occultic/satanic literature

- Bible, Psalms, or New Testament (used for ritualistic backward reading)
- school essays on occult topics: death, sacrifice, violence
- occultic paraphernalia: robe, silver chalice, goblet, sword, oddly shaped knives, black candles, bone collection
- pentagrams
- a Book of Shadows (a satanist's personal diary of satanic activities)
- obvious behavioral changes
- new set of friends
- signs of self-mutilation such as occult symbols carved or tattooed into the skin
- a satanic nickname
- a new interest in buying jewelry with occult designs
- chronic depression
- obsessive interest in heavy metal music, black clothes, accumulation of power
- preoccupation with death
- nightmares about demons
- hallucinations about hearing voices

What should you do if you think someone you know is dabbling in satanism? First, make a list of all warning signs the person is showing. Second, find someone in your community who, through the list, can interpret the dabbler's level of involvement. People who might be able to help include ministers, police officers, mental health professionals, youth leaders, and social workers. Third, have someone familiar with satanism help you confront the dabbler.

The dabbler will most likely need extended, biblically based counseling. The person might even need hospitalization. And in some rare instances the dabbler might need a prayer of exorcism.

I believe satanic hexes and rituals cannot touch or disturb a child of God. And I believe the power of God is greater than the power of Satan. First John 4:4 is true: "You, dear children, are from God ... the one who is in you is greater than the one who is in the world."

Jesus "disarmed the powers and authorities, he made a public spectacle of them, triumphing over them by the cross" (Colossians 2:15).

After conquering Satan, Jesus held him up as a whipped loser. In Christ we share that victory.

13

The Appeal of Christianity

By RONALD ENROTH

Ronald Enroth, who also wrote chapter 1, is professor of sociology at Westmont College, Santa Barbara, Calif., and author of several books about cults.

CULTS grow in the soil of the church's failure.

Many searchers for spiritual truth end up in cults because they believe the Christian church is lifeless and cold, hopelessly inflexible, and out of step with a changing world.

But that's not the real church. Not the church based on the heart of the gospel. The Church of Jesus Christ is full of excitement, dynamism, and relevance to life. But the average unbeliever doesn't know this.

We need to do a better job of telling people what authentic Christianity is really like.

One of the most revolutionary messages we have for our world today—a message that will draw people to Christianity—is the good news that God himself has visited this small planet. This is one of the most important facts in all of human history. People who witnessed this incredible event became so excited they went out to tell the world.

This is the starting point of Christianity. And it is this astounding event, perhaps more than anything else, that compels people to decide whether the Christian faith is true or false.

WE CAN KNOW GOD

The excitement of Christianity comes not only from the fact that we are living on a visited planet. We can actually know this God who inserted himself into human history.

The God of the Bible is personal. He is not an impersonal force or an abstract principle, as some religions teach. He is not a distant Father who is unconcerned about the daily lives of His children.

This is an issue we need to communicate to our non-believing friends. God not only exists but also is near. And we can approach Him.

Former New Ager Elliot Miller described his experience of coming to know the God of Scripture.

"I no longer just knew *about* Him—I *knew* Him. I found this intimate fellowship with Christ to be the sweetest thing I'd ever known in life. It surpassed the 'bliss' of cosmic consciousness—which I had previously thought to be the ultimate experience" (*A Crash Course on the New Age Movement*, Baker Book House).

One of the greatest pluses of the Christian faith is that God is personal. Eastern religions and New Age cults see God as an impersonal force. It is tough to have a relationship with a force.

The idea of a personal God is central to Christianity. Christianity is far more than one of the world's great faiths. It is the revelation of divine love expressed in a person, Jesus Christ, who is God's gift of truth to humanity.

This is clear enough in John 3:16. "For God so loved the world that he gave his one and only Son, that whoever believes in him shall not perish but have eternal life." Romans 5:8 is another passage that tells us of God giving us himself. "But God demonstrates his own love for us in this: While we were still sinners, Christ died for us."

THE HONEST RELIGION

That brings us to another attraction of Christianity. It's honest. It tells us what we already know in our hearts.

We have all sinned.

Compare that view of humanity's fallen nature with some of the cults that deny the existence of sin.

I once read this in an advertisement for the Vedanta Press and Bookshop in Hollywood: "It is a sin to call anyone a sinner. It is a standing libel on human nature. Vedanta does not believe in sin, only error, and the greatest error is to think you are weak."

The God of the Bible is a truth-telling God. In reaching out to people in cults and new religions, we need to help them see that God is more on target in describing human nature as "desperately wicked" (Jeremiah 17:9, KJV).

Sin is real, not an illusion. Eastern mystics, New Agers, and believers in Christian Science all proclaim sin does not exist. Yet the Bible declares, "If we claim to be without sin, we deceive ourselves and the truth is not in us" (1 John 1:8).

Almalee Woody attended the Christian Science church for 23 years. But one day she attended a Bible study with Christian friends and became a born-again Christian herself.

"It was there that I confronted the glaring and awful truth that I was a sinner," she wrote in *Christian Way Newsletter.*

"I had truly been believing that I was the 'perfect child of God.' Oh, how very hard it was to face this fact! I struggled with it to the point of even arguing with our teacher about this. He lovingly pointed out to me Romans 3:23, 'For all have sinned and fall short of the glory of God.' I remember stating that I hadn't. He was rather surprised at this. Then he gently pursued by asking me if I thought I was without sin. I replied that I believed I was. He rephrased his question and asked me if I thought I was as sinless as Jesus Christ. Well, that was a different matter. I could see how very imperfect I was compared to Jesus Christ. I began to comprehend that sin was more than just breaking the Ten Commandments. How naive I had been on the subject of sin."

We're not God. Not only does biblical Christianity present us with a personal God and the truth of our sinful nature, but also it denies a notion so common in cultic religion. This is the notion that we are God or have the potential to become God.

The made-for-TV movie of Shirley MacLaine's autobiography, *Out on a Limb,* shows the actress standing on the beach at Malibu. Beside her stands her New Age teacher. He instructs her to "look within" for the truth. Then, together, they face the Pacific with outstretched arms, and they repeat over and over, "I am God. I am God."

To the Christian this is blasphemous. We are the created, not the Creator. Humanity is not divine; nor is it possible to "merge" with God through yoga, chanting, or any other psycho-spiritual technique. Yet, in today's spiritual supermarket, there are many sincere seekers who believe they can attain godhood.

One such person was Bob Burrows. With just a superficial understanding of Christianity he concluded that Eastern religions held a purer spirituality. He said he thought all religions, though externally different, were basically the same and were headed in the same direction. Bob's goal was to achieve divine status.

"When confronted by the God of the Bible," he said, "convictions about my divinity evaporated. Divine attributes seemed fitting only when applied to Him. I don't know how I could have thought I was all-powerful, all-knowing, or omnipresent. I obviously was not. I simply was not God. My aspiration to deity was unmasked as the outrageous but pathetic pretense it was. Like Adam and Eve, I felt naked and ashamed."*

One important appeal of Christianity is that Jesus can lift the burden of sin and guilt when we turn to Him in confession and repentance. We need not try to become God, or search in vain for evidence of our inner divinity. When we bow before Christ in joyful submission, we begin a pilgrimage toward true freedom and meaning.

NO SECRET RITUALS

False religion is a religion of concealment, of secrecy. Biblical Christianity is a religion in which God has revealed, not concealed. This is an important point to stress when reaching out to people involved in Eastern religions, occult groups, or the Mormon church.

For example, unless you are a Mormon in good standing, you cannot enter a Mormon Temple or participate in the secret rites that are performed inside.

But in Christian churches there are no hidden truths or secret rituals. For us, the secret is out: Jesus Christ is Lord.

"God has allowed us to know the secret of his plan, and it is this: he purposed long ago in his sovereign will that all human history should be consummated in Christ, that everything that exists in Heaven or earth should find its perfection and fulfilment in him. In Christ we have been given an inheritance . . . So that we, in due time, as the first to put our hope

---

*From the Spiritual Counterfeits Project newsletter, winter 1984-85. The Spiritual Counterfeits Projects is a nonprofit, Christian organization that researches new religions, especially those based on Eastern philosophies.

in Christ, may bring praise to his glory!" (Ephesians 1:9-12, Phillips).

We can know "the mystery that has been kept hidden for ages and generations, but is now disclosed to the saints . . . which is Christ in you, the hope of glory" (Colossians 1:26-27).

Christianity continues to attract converts because it is a religion of hope. Christians do not look forward to endless cycles of reincarnation, or merger with some vaguely defined cosmic consciousness, or extinction.

One final thought.

It is important to expose errors in cults and other non-Christian religions. But we must also be willing to engage in self-criticism and make certain that we, too, do not fall victim to cultic snares.

As you have read through this book, you have probably noticed some similarities between Christianity and other religions. That's partly because others are borrowing from Christianity. But we need to be careful not to borrow from them any ideas that clash with God's Word revealed in Scripture.

Christians must not only work to develop skills for telling the difference between false religion and authentic Christianity but also show the world that we have a vibrant testimony to offer.

We haven't always done a good job of presenting Christianity as an exciting and relevant religion. We have better answers than others do to the really important questions of life. But we haven't always made that obvious.

With God's help, we can.

APPENDIX

RELIGIONS OLD AND NEW: A COMPARATIVE CHART

By MATT ZAHNISER

TOPIC	MORMONS	JEHOVAH'S WITNESSES	ISLAM
GOD	Is married, was once a man. Has a father who is god over another world. Humans can become a god.	Jehovah is one, not three in one. Holy Spirit is not a person, but a force.	One sovereign Lord, transcendent, cannot be known.
JESUS	Spirit brother of Lucifer. Is now a deity, one of many gods, and our "elder brother."	Not divine. Once the angel Michael. On earth was just a man. Rose only in spirit.	A prophet like Muhammad. Virgin-born. Not crucified, not God's Son.
SACRED WRITINGS	*The Book of Mormon; The Pearl of Great Price; The Doctrine and Covenants;* and the Bible (least reliable).	*New World Translation of the Holy Scriptures*	Qur'an (Koran). Secondary, Hadith (sayings and deeds of Muhammad). The Bible is corrupt and unreliable.
SIN/ SALVATION	We become worthy through good works.	144,000 "elect" will be saved through Jesus. Nonelect must earn salvation.	Humans are fallible, fickle, and need guidance, not salvation. Rewards and punishment decided by God, based on human works and divine mercy.
LIFE AFTER DEATH	After death but before Judgment Day, the wicked get a second chance. Four levels of destiny. (1) Highest are members of LDS church. (2) Good people but not LDS. (3) Unrighteous. (4) Lucifer, his angels, and the unrepentant "sons of perdition."	The lost will face annihilation. The 144,000 are being resurrected spiritually to heaven. Other Witnesses will be resurrected to an earthly life of endless bliss if they are faithful.	Eternal hell awaits those who reject Islam or do not live according to the light they have. Those who are saved will live forever in Paradise. Hell and heaven will be experienced in resurrected, physical bodies.
SPIRITUAL PRACTICES	Abstain from alcohol, tobacco, coffee, and tea. Spiritual support through age and gender groups. Sunday School, and priesthood groups. Temple rituals, meetinghouse worship and study.	Don't observe religious and secular holidays. Celebrate "Lord's Evening Meal" once a year. Attend Sunday worship. Have several study meetings each week.	Pray five times daily. Fast during month of Ramadan. Share wealth with the needy. Pilgrimage to Mecca once in life.

TOPIC	BUDDHISM/NICHIREN SHOSHU	HINDUISM/KRISHNA	UNITY
GOD	Some worship Buddha as lord. Most worship impersonal deities they call "forces."	A divine force, known through Krishna instead of Christ. Other Hindus believe God is impersonal. Still others believe in many gods.	Is the only power in the universe. This power is good, impersonal.
JESUS	Has no place in this religion.	A spiritually enlightened person, an earthly appearance of God. Some Hindus make no provision for Christ at all.	Was no more divine than other humans. He simply became aware of His divinity as can all humans.
SACRED WRITINGS	*Lotus Sutra.* When a phrase containing the essence of this book is chanted, good things happen, including salvation.	Vedas Upanishads, *Bhagavad Gita, Shrimad Bhagavatam,* and many other writings.	The Bible is respected, but not as final and authoritative. Respects scriptures of other faiths.
SIN/ SALVATION	Salvation comes from devotion to the *Lotus Sutra* and chanting. Salvation includes deliverance from all barriers to good health, happiness, a new world order, and union with Buddha.	By chanting the name Hare Krishna and serving him in total devotion, humans are saved from further reincarnations.	Salvation is not through repentance. It is through realizing Christ already dwells in us. Everyone will reach this point eventually.
LIFE AFTER DEATH	Teaches reincarnation. People can reach impersonal union with Buddha.	Unenlightened people will be reborn on earth or in one of the many heavens and hells. Those immersed in Krishna consciousness will become one with him.	No literal hell. No heaven. People are reincarnated until they reach oneness with God, as Jesus did.
SPIRITUAL PRACTICES	Three important ones: (1) chanting the Daimoko, a phrase that is the essence of *Lotus Sutra;* (2) worship before the Gohonzon, a scroll containing the Daimoko; and (3) Kaidon, pilgrimage to world headquarters on Mount Fuji.	Worship approved images. Chanting, offerings, study of texts, begging, yoga. Most important is public chanting of Hare Krishna mantra.	Worship services with instruction and community support. 24-hour prayer ministry.

TOPIC	NEW AGE	TRANSCENDENTAL MEDITATION	UNIFICATION CHURCH (MOONIES)
GOD	Is impersonal, like the "Force" in *Star Wars*. Humans are gods who don't know it.	The inner self of every person is divine, part of the impersonal "God."	One personal God. Has dual characteristics of masculine and feminine. Is not part of a Trinity.
JESUS	Esteemed as a great teacher, spiritual master, and guru. Was no more divine than other humans.	Like all persons, Jesus had a divine essence. Unlike most, He discovered it.	A perfect human whom God chose to be Messiah. Failed his mission to find a second Eve and start a perfect family. Is not the eternal Son.
SACRED WRITINGS	No holy book. Interested in selected Bible passages, *I Ching*, Hindu, Buddhist, and Taoist writings, as well as many works on astrology, mysticism, magic.	Writings of Maharishi, founder of TM, especially his commentary on the Hindu scripture, *Bhagavad-Gita*,	The Bible, Sun Myung Moon's *Divine Principle*, and Moon's sermons.
SIN/ SALVATION	People need to discover they are divine. The path to enlightenment is through self-awareness and occult practices, such as channeling (communicating with the spirit world).	Humans are not sinful but have forgotten their inner divinity. Commitment to a guru and practice of meditation bring knowledge of the inner self.	The Fall came from Eve having sex with Lucifer. Humans atone for sin through good works. Ultimate redemption will come from True Parents (Moon and his wife). Moon completes the mission Jesus failed.
LIFE AFTER DEATH	Reincarnations occur until person reaches oneness with God. No eternal life as a resurrected person.	Reincarnation, followed by loss of personality in a final union of the self with the divine reality called Brahman.	Everyone will be saved.
SPIRITUAL PRACTICES	The variety includes yoga, meditation, astrology, and channeling.	An initiation rite. Mentally recite mantras (secret words or syllables) twice daily, 20 minutes each time. Postures and breathing exercises of yoga are gradually added.	Moon chooses wedding partners. Mass weddings every few years (6,516 couples wed in 1988). Have "pledge" services to renew vows on the first day of each week, month, year, and holy days. Worship on holy days. Use holy salt for spiritual cleansing.

TOPIC	SCIENTOLOGY	SATANISM	CHRISTIANITY
GOD	Many gods exist. Humans can become gods, called "operating thetans."	God exists as a universal, impersonal force who does not care about humans. Satan represents the ultimate force with which to reckon.	Is personal, eternal, all-powerful. Revealed to humans as Father, Son, and Holy Spirit.
JESUS	Jesus was an Essene who believed in reincarnation. The Crucifixion is a legend.	Jesus is the enemy, the target of Satan's designs. Satan is the personal savior.	Second person of Godhead. Virgin-born. Died for sins of humanity, rose again, ascended to heaven.
SACRED WRITINGS	*Dianetics: The Modern Science of Mental Health*, by L. Ron Hubbard.	Anton La Vey's *Satanic Bible*.	Bible
SIN/ SALVATION	Humans are spirit beings with many past lives. Bad experiences in past lives cause problems and hang-ups (engrams) in present lives. Salvation involves getting clear of engrams, being released from the cycle of reincarnation, and becoming an operating thetan (god).	Salvation means being free of moral scruples and having power over one's own destiny and the destiny of others.	All have sinned. All who repent and confess Jesus as Lord will be saved.
LIFE AFTER DEATH	People who get "clear" of engrams become operating thetans, immortal spirits with unlimited powers.	Offers no clear teaching about life after death. Some believe they will rule in hell with Satan.	All will be judged by God. The righteous will enjoy everlasting life, the unrighteous will suffer eternal separation from God.
SPIRITUAL PRACTICES	Devotees wanting to become "clear" work with an "auditor," who leads them on a spiritual journey to erase the effects of engrams. Weekly worship according to the book of *Ceremonies*. Observe the birth of the founder and anniversary of the publication of *Dianetics*.	Black Mass imitates the Roman Catholic Mass. Rituals help people accept their carnal side without guilt. Ritual cursing of enemies. Sexual rituals observed on 10 satanic holidays. Blood sacrifices, even human sacrifices, are authorized by the *Satanic Bible*.	Prayer, reading the Bible, worshiping God in weekly church services, rituals of baptism and the Lord's Supper.

Matt Zahniser is professor of world religions, Asbury Theological Seminary, Wilmore, Ky.